D1296566

This book is a gift for your hopeful heart that wants to adopt more than anything in the world, but doesn't know where to start.

In these pages, we hope you find the information you need to take the first steps in your journey, and the inspiration to help you believe that dreams really do come true.

WELCOME!
GREAT IDEAS ARE AHEAD.

THIS BOOK IS FOR YOU no matter how you are connected to the world of adoption. Perhaps you are just starting the journey to finding a match and growing your family through adoption. Maybe you are an adoption professional looking for more resources and information for your clients. You may know of a friend or family member who has been waiting for a child and you are looking for ways to help. Whatever your connection to adoption, we're excited to share the ideas in this book with you! You will find real-life stories from folks who have already adopted and lots of great, usable ideas you can implement right away to smooth out the next steps in your journey.

We have been working on this book for quite a while to make sure it contains actionable outreach ideas, accurate and complete user guides and real-life experience from other adoptive families. We have worked with several adoption professionals to make sure you can rely on the information we share in this book. It is our goal that *The Essential Guide to Adoption Outreach* will be a trusted resource you can use to help navigate the road ahead with confidence and inspiration.

TABLE OF CONTENTS

GETTING STARTED

ADOPTION OUTREACH IDEAS

SOCIAL MEDIA

SOCIAL MEDIA CONT.

NEXT STEPS

FIRST CONTACT

LAWS BY STATE

IN CLOSING

THROUGHOUT THE BOOK

FOLLOW THE FOOTPRINTS FOR REAL STORIES AND ADVICE FROM FAMILIES WHO HAVE BEEN IN YOUR SHOES.

LOOK THROUGH THE MAGNIFYING GLASS TO FIND PROFESSIONAL EXPERIENCE AND ADVICE.

GREAT IDEAS ARE NOTED WITH LIGHTBULBS. THESE ARE HELPFUL HINTS YOU WON'T WANT TO MISS.

FOLLOW "MARIO AND MARIA" AS AN EXAMPLE OF HOW TO SET UP YOUR OUTREACH MATERIALS.

PIECE BY PIECE YOUR FAMILY WILL BE BUILT AS YOU COMPLETE THE PUZZLE OF ADOPTION OUTREACH.

NOTES:

WELCOME

TOPICS COVERED IN THIS SECTION:

- Different Types of Adoption
- Completing a Home Study
- The Need for Outreach & Outreach Plans
- The Importance of Personal Branding
- Why & How to Use Keywords
- Tips for Setting Up Contact Methods

WELCOME!

You are entering the world of adoption.

AS YOU BEGIN ***to navigate the world of adoption, the first choice you need to make is regarding the type of adoption you would like to pursue. That decision will lead you down a path that is, of course, filled with lots of other important choices, but this first choice is paramount and will dictate your next steps. We will very briefly outline the different options available to you and how each affects your need to do outreach.***

AGENCY OR ATTORNEY-ASSISTED ADOPTION

In this type of adoption, an agency or attorney does outreach for you to find an expectant family. An agency may place ads that reach out to expectant parents considering adoption and then, after counseling and screening, they present profiles of hopeful adoptive parents to the expectant parents to review. Your wait time may vary based on a multitude of factors, including how many expectant parents the agency works with and how many hopeful adoptive parents are in the pool. An attorney may advertise on your behalf and help you connect with expectant parents. They typically do not work with a pool of expectant parents, but rather help you match with an expectant parent through advertising or networking. State laws dictate advertising rules. In some states only agencies can advertise, in others only attorneys and in some states only the adoptive family can advertise. Please speak with an attorney in your state to determine what is legal and appropriate.

NOTE: We list state laws on pages 118-127; however, please check with an attorney in your state to confirm your state laws. Laws may change and the interpretation of laws may change over time as well. While we share the current state laws at the time of printing, we are not attorneys and cannot offer legal advice.

IDENTIFIED ADOPTION

If you have connected with an expectant parent through your own outreach, your agency or attorney will perform the necessary steps for you to complete the adoption. If you were already working with an agency when this connection was made, often you do not have to pay the match fee, just the legal and administrative fees. This can save you a good deal of money in the adoption process. Be sure to ask your agency or attorney how their fees change if you bring a match to the agency vs. them finding a match for you.

INDEPENDENT ADOPTION

In an independent or private adoption, you implement all of the outreach needed to find an expectant mother and then your attorney or agency completes the state-mandated counseling and legal work for the adoption. Independent adoptions are primarily, but not exclusively, done with adoption attorneys. You typically budget a larger amount for advertising and outreach since the agency or attorney is not performing this service for you. You should definitely have a strong social media presence in addition to advertising in this case. You will need to have a home study completed before beginning your outreach, and you will still need to work with an attorney or agency. Which one you need to work with is determined by your state laws.

FOSTER CARE

The process of adopting from foster care is not covered in this book. This process varies, not only by state, but by county. Since adopting from foster care is regulated by state and county guidelines, please consult with your local Department of Health and Family Services (DHFS) office.

INTERNATIONAL

Inter-country or international adoptions have fallen in popularity for 11 straight years. In 2015 there were only just over 6,000 completed international adoptions, down from a high of 22,000 in 2004. There are many reasons for this decline, and the upswing in private adoptions in America is certainly one of them.

FIRST STEPS

An interview with Amy Imber about completing a home study for your adoption.

BEFORE YOU CAN ADOPT, *you need to complete a home study with an adoption professional which certifies that you are eligible to adopt. If you are just starting your adoption journey, you might have a lot of questions or even some fears about completing a home study. Amy Imber from Connecting Hearts Adoption Services provided the following insights about the types of information that is gathered during a home study, and gives some helpful hints for efficiently and confidently completing your home study.*

WHEN IS A HOME STUDY REQUIRED?

In the United States, anyone looking to adopt a non-relative child age 17 or younger is required to have a home study. It is typically filed with the courts and, in short, it is a document that approves someone to be eligible to adopt.

A home study contains all sorts of information about you, the prospective adoptive parent(s), including personal inventories, background checks and financial statements. Your home study professional will review all the documents you provide, interview you individually and as a couple and then produce a document called a Home Study that approves you to adopt.

Although it varies from state to state, you can expect the information collected to include the following:

- Information about your family of origin (parents and siblings.)
- Where you grew up.
- Family traditions.
- Your religious beliefs, if any. How you intend to incorporate your belief system with your adopted child.
- How you met your spouse and what endears you to him/her. Something you would change in your marriage, if given a chance. How long you dated before you married. When and where you married.
- Child care plans once you bring your child home.
- Why you are adopting.
- How you feel about parenting and discipline.
- Why you think children are placed for adoption. Whether you plan to tell your child he/she is adopted and if so, when.
- How you feel about post adoption contact with birth parents.

You will also need to provide information and documentation for the following:

- Previous marriages/divorces.
- Medical history (you will need current physicals.)
- Background checks with local, state and federal officials as well as child protective services.
- Income and monthly expenses. Does your income exceed your expenses?
- Employment and salary verification.
- Information regarding health insurance and life insurance.
- Copies of documents such as Driver's Licenses, Marriage License(s), Divorce Decrees and taxes.

(continued on next page)

▲ *Amy getting to enjoy the best part of her job—new babies!*

(Completing a Home Study—continued from page 7)

Lastly, you will be asked to provide letters of reference from family, friends and members of your faith community, if applicable.

The home study process could include both home and office visits with a social worker. These requirements vary from state to state, so be sure to ask your home study provider what to expect.

The list goes on and on! All of this information (plus more!) is collected and written into a report that hopefully approves you to be eligible to adopt!

IS IT HARD TO PASS A HOME STUDY?

Honestly, most people can get an approved home study. There are disqualifying factors and those vary from state to state. If you have something in your background that concerns you, discuss this with a social worker. Your social worker is not there to find problems, rather they are on your team and want this to happen for you and your family. They should be a support to you and one of your biggest cheerleaders!

WHO CAN PERFORM A HOME STUDY?

The guidelines regarding the people who can help you with a home study vary from state to state. Your adoption agency might perform home studies, or you can hire an independent home study professional who is a Licensed Clinical Social Worker. Since you can adopt in your state or anywhere across the country, it is important for you to partner with someone who can complete a study that will work for you, no matter where you take it! If you go through an agency, you want to confirm they are a licensed agency. Any licensed agency should be able to easily provide you with a copy of their license.

HOW SHOULD I PREPARE FOR IT?

Your home study provider will give you a list of documents she/he will need to complete your home study. Some of these take longer to get than others, so begin right away. Be sure to read the list carefully so you understand what needs to be notarized, which documents need to be originals and which can be copies or print-outs.

There is not much else to do to prepare for the home visit. Everyone will say, "Just be yourself!" and while it is a cliché, it is absolutely true. It is important to be honest and open when meeting with your social worker. She is not looking for perfection and, believe it or not, there is no white glove test! Your social worker is there to make sure your home is safe and suitable for children.

HOW LONG DOES IT TAKE TO FINISH?

The amount of time it takes to complete a study varies from state to state. Some states require multiple home visits or adoption education courses before completing a study. Some states use electronic fingerprinting, which helps expedite the process, while other states use paper fingerprint cards that have to be mailed in and processed. Your home study provider should be able to give you an expectation of how long the home study will take to complete, but a general range is three weeks to three months.

DO I "OWN" MY HOME STUDY AND IS IT TRANSFERABLE?

This is at the discretion of the provider you work with and, in some cases, the state. Yes, some home study providers believe you "own" your study and will give you everything you need so that you have the greatest flexibility in your future adoption possibilities. Whether or not an agency will give you your study to be used outside of their office is at their discretion, so be sure to ask if this is important to you! In a perfect adoption world, you want to "own" your study along with the supporting documents so you can take it where ever you like. In addition, some states may not allow you to have a copy of your study. Some states require a study be approved by a court before it is released. Having a home study that can be transferred to (and accepted by) a different agency can be important down the road in your adoption journey, so be sure to ask your home study provider up front if this is a possibility.

WHAT ARE POST-PLACEMENT VISITS?

Post-placement visits are often required in order for a person or family to finalize their adoption. Often the same provider that completed your home study will complete your post-placement visits. Once you bring your child home, your social worker will meet with you, often at your home, to gather information for the post-placement report. You can expect the following questions during a post-placement visit:

- How has your child adjusted to their new home? How is your adjustment to parenthood?
- What is your child's schedule for sleep and feeding? What types of food/formula do you provide? Any likes or dislikes so far?
- How have you celebrated becoming parents? What response have you received from friends and family?
- What are your child's growth measurements such as weight, length and/or height?
- Who is your pediatrician and when has your child been to the doctor?
- Are you happy? Are you tired? The last two answers are likely YES and YES!

WHAT SHOULD I LOOK FOR IN A HOME STUDY PROVIDER?

It is best to look for a home study provider who makes you feel comfortable, is experienced and is someone you can trust. You will be sharing A LOT of personal and private information about yourself with someone you do not know well, so being comfortable with someone is a must! It is always best to work with a referral from a friend, adoption professional or family member. There are support groups across the United States and many adoptive families are willing to share their experience with home study providers. The home study is often one of the first fees a family will pay in the adoption process, so you also want to choose a provider with competitive fees. Let's face it, adoption is expensive!

Amy Imber is the Executive Director of Connecting Hearts Adoption Services in Orlando, Florida. Her agency has been serving prospective adoptive families across the state of Florida since 2008.

Connecting Hearts Adoption Services is an agency that only provides the home study service. Connecting Hearts Adoption Services families take their studies across Florida and across the country successfully adopting!

Contact: connectingheartsadoption.com or call 407-733-8642

THE NEED FOR OUTREACH

Why is it so important?

WHAT IS ADOPTION OUTREACH *and why is it important? Adoption outreach is actively building a network of connections that can further your search for a match with expectant parents. This network can begin with people who already love and support you, like your family and friends, and can grow to include people you meet within your local community as well as on social media. There are several types of adoption, as we discussed earlier and whichever path is right for you, outreach can make a meaningful impact on your journey.*

Adoption outreach makes sense no matter what type of adoption you are planning. In an agency or attorney-assisted adoption, doing your own outreach can save you both time and money. Even in traditional agency programs, the fees are usually discounted if you match through your own efforts.

Many agencies encourage their clients to do outreach and networking, and may even have resources available to help. Your agency or attorney will also have the most up-to-date information on state laws that may apply to your outreach efforts.

If you are planning an independent adoption, without the assistance of finding a match through an agency, your attorney or agency may have guidelines for you to consider, but you are often encouraged to just "get the word out" that you are adopting. This book outlines a step-by-step process to do that efficiently and effectively.

Whether you are supplementing your agency's outreach by doing some of your own legwork or embarking on a comprehensive outreach plan, this book will make the process as easy as possible and you might even have fun doing it! Since there is a lot of information to cover, let's get started!!

▲ Laura and Kara meeting their son for the first time!

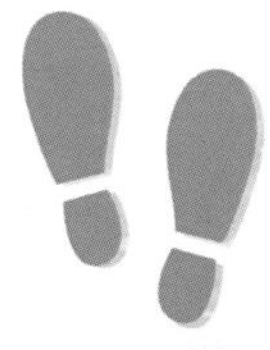

ACTUAL CLIENT STORY:
LAURA & KARA

WE WERE OFFICIALLY "ON THE BOOKS" STARTING IN NOVEMBER OF 2012 *and were contacted by our son's birth mom a few months later. She received over a hundred family profiles that fit her criteria. At first, she kept putting our profile to the side as we seemed too far away geographically. She then went on our Facebook page where she was hooked by how we came alive through social media.*

She loved our YouTube video, our active adoption Facebook page and our website. She was able to see how and with whom her son would live. We were excited when she chose us to parent Vincent, who was born in May 2013. We enjoy a very special relationship with Vincent's birth parents and his extended birth family. Open adoption was the best decision for all of us.

DIFFERENT OUTREACH PLANS

How much work do you want to take on?

WE WILL COVER ***different types of outreach and different ways to build your networking community, with the goal of connecting with an expectant family who is considering adoption. It's easy to feel overwhelmed as you get started but don't worry, you will be a pro in no time! Take a little time and think about how much time, energy and money you want to invest in your adoption outreach and then take it one step at a time.***

The amount of outreach you choose to do may vary depending on whether you're supplementing your agency's outreach or pursuing an independent adoption where you will be responsible for all of your own outreach efforts. Below are some suggestions for different levels of outreach you may consider:

- Light and Easy
- Working It
- The Whole Nine Yards

▲ Laura and Kara's matching Facebook page, personal website and outreach cards ready for action!

LIGHT AND EASY:

Create a Facebook page to use for both outreach and updating family and friends as your adoption journey unfolds. Get some outreach cards printed to use in your day-to-day life and create a webpage with Hopefully Parents so you have an online presence where you can direct expectant parents.

WORKING IT:

Create a Facebook page, as well as other social media accounts, specifically for your adoption outreach instead of using personal accounts you already have. Actively post regular updates and seek out other adoption-related pages to "like" and comment on. Distribute pull-tab flyers around your community or any place you might visit. Create a webpage on hopefullyparents.com that includes a video and photo gallery. Regularly check out our Bright Ideas blog on HopefullyParents.com for creative tips and new ideas to implement in your outreach plans.

THE WHOLE NINE YARDS:

Build a custom website complete with links to several social media accounts. Post content regularly on your social media accounts and keep your website updated. Make sure to "work" social media accounts by "liking" and "sharing" content at least 5 days a week. Send outreach letters to family and friends, as well as medical offices, campus health centers, crisis pregnancy centers, etc. Set up Google Ads to direct even more traffic to your website and social media accounts. Another option to increase your exposure is to use a service like Parent Profiles at Adoption.com. Although it can be expensive it's a great option to ensure you're getting the most exposure possible!

NOTE: For more information on advertising and solicitation, please refer to pages 118-127 in this book. Hopefully Parents always recommends checking with your attorney before starting any form of advertising.

YOUR BRAND

It is really important to use branding for your outreach.

BRANDS ARE FAMILIAR *and that is why a lot of companies spend so much time and money to create and reinforce their brand. Branding is creating a logo, tagline, etc. to define your company and your product to your audience. Once you have your brand created, you use your logo, tagline, etc. in everything you make from business cards to billboards. Think about using the same approach for your adoption outreach. It might sound more complicated or gimmicky than it really is. Personal branding is just another way to describe the consistent message that you want other people to receive. That's how simple it really is!*

CREATE YOUR BRAND

Branding is what companies use to create a feeling about their company, product or service. Johnson & Johnson wants us to think of them as a family-friendly and trusted provider of products for home and baby. They work hard to cultivate that image by striving for consistency in every media portrayal of their products. Chances are, when you see the Johnson & Johnson logo, you think of sweet babies fresh out of the bath smelling like lavender and chamomile.

Creating a personal brand is a critical first step in adoption outreach! You want to create a brand for all of your adoption outreach so that, over time, people come to know you and know what to expect from you. Think of it as your reputation or your image. Everything you do online should be representative of a singular image that defines you. If you have wildly different branding across different platforms (Facebook, Instagram, Pinterest, etc), people will be unsure of who you are, and it will prevent people from feeling connected to you. Networking on social media platforms comes down to creating connections, so branding is incredibly important.

Decide who you are and how you want to be perceived, use your keywords (more on those soon) and stay consistent. This is the story of YOU, so take some time to define that story before you begin. Choosing your brand will make your story stronger and build authenticity.

CONSISTENCY & TRUST

These are the most important aspects of your brand! If your social media accounts show lots of pictures of you playing video games with your friends and eating junk food but your adoption profile says you love being active in the outdoors and eating healthy food, expectant parents will get confused about who the "real you" is. Being consistent with your message when you engage in any sort of outreach is vital to creating trust and reinforcing who you will be as an adoptive parent or family.

KEYWORDS

Keywords and branding go hand in hand and are the building blocks of your brand. On page 14, we will go into details on exactly what keywords are and how to use them. The important thing to note is that as you select and use keywords they should remain consistent with your branding. Anyone viewing your outreach materials should always receive a consistent message about who you are.

MARIO AND MARIA

√ Selected this photo for their profile picture.

√ Set up all their accounts on Facebook, Twitter and Instagram.

√ Picked keywords to use on their social media sites and their website.

▲ *Taking time to develop your brand will make a powerful and positive impact!*

SOCIAL MEDIA ACCOUNTS

It's a great idea to set up all social media accounts at one time, even if you don't plan on using them. This way, you can be sure that the username or account name remains the same on the different platforms. If a name isn't available on one platform, you can think of a different one to use on all the accounts before you go "live." Your goal is just to keep it simple and consistent so people can easily find you.

Imagine using "MarioMariaAdopting" for your blog and Twitter account but then noticing that this name isn't available on Facebook. You would need to select a different name like "MarioMariaAdoptionJourney" and then you would be using two different names, which is confusing. This is why you want to use the same name across the different platforms as much as you can.

COVER PHOTO/PROFILE PHOTO

We recommend choosing the same photo for your profile picture on all your social media accounts. If you are planning on creating an adoption profile (or already have one), this should be the same photo that is on your adoption profile cover page. This is an easy way to make sure a great photo of you is the first thing people see so they will recognize you when visiting your website, Facebook page, Instagram, etc.

BECOME AN EXPERT IN POSTING WITH THIS QUICK REFERENCE GUIDE TO PHOTO IMAGE SIZING!
(DIMENSION UNITS ARE IN PIXELS)

FACEBOOK

- **COVER PHOTO** – 828 x 464
- **PROFILE PHOTO** – 360 x 360
- **APP/TAB IMAGE** – 111 x 74
- **LINK IMAGE** – 1200 x 628
- **PHOTO POST** – 940 x 788

TWITTER

- **HEADER** – 1500 x 500
- **PROFILE PHOTO** – 500 x 500
- **TWEETED IMAGE** – 1024 x 1024

PINTEREST

- **PROFILE PHOTO** – 600 x 600
- **PINS** – 736 x 1104
- **BOARD COVER** – 736 x 498

INSTAGRAM

- **PROFILE PHOTO** – 180 x 180
- **PHOTO POST** – 1080 x 1080

YOUTUBE

- **CHANNEL ART** – 2560 x 1440
- **VIDEO THUMBNAIL** – 1280 x 720
- **CHANNEL ICON** – 800 x 800

KEYWORDS

What are keywords and how do you use them?

WHAT DO THEY DO? ***A lot of people know the term "keyword" but aren't aware of their importance and how they can really benefit someone in their adoption outreach. Let's explore what keywords are, why they are so important for every aspect of your adoption outreach and how to figure out which keywords to use.***

WHAT ARE KEYWORDS?

A keyword is a word or phrase that you intentionally and consistently use throughout your social media platforms and websites/blogs. Search engines look for keywords when deciding what websites or pages they will show when someone enters search terms.

WHY DOES IT MATTER?

Using your keywords in the first few sentences of your website, and then again several times in the rest of your website text, will increase your search engine results and your potential to connect with an expectant family. Repetition of keywords throughout your website, adoption profile, outreach materials and social media sites will create consistency for your adoption brand.

It is important to take a little time to generate a list of keywords that are important to your adoption outreach journey. Remember, a keyword is not limited to one word. It can also be a short phrase of 3 to 5 words.

IN TOTAL, YOU WILL PROBABLY NEED ABOUT 6-10 KEYWORDS OR KEY PHRASES THAT YOU CAN USE THROUGHOUT YOUR ADOPTION OUTREACH.

WHERE TO START

Review key aspects of your life to discover what words describe you and your partner. Select keywords that describe you as both an individual and as a couple. Use this list of subjects below to help you brainstorm keywords and then narrow your list down to 6-10 keywords that you can use in all of your outreach:

- Location:
  Beach, Los Angeles, Midwest, Big Apple, four seasons.
- Hobbies:
  Vegetarian cooking, classic cars, international travel, state parks, snowboarding, hunting, boating, gardening.
- Art, Music and Leisure:
  Opera, crafts, bluegrass music, art gallery, mystery novels, fashion, DIY home shows, antiques, vinyl records.
- Sports and Games:
  NFL teams, skateboarding, Dungeons & Dragons, volleyball league, family board game night, trivia champ.
- Health and Fitness:
  Triathlon, 5K runner, spin class, solo hikes, swimmer, gym rat, nature walks, organic cooking, scratch recipes.
- Family Values & Religion:
  Family dinners, prayer circles, stay-at-home parent.

HASHTAGS

Once you have established your keywords, these will be the building blocks of your brand and adoption outreach. An easy way to incorporate your keywords on your social media accounts is to turn them into hashtags. Every time you post a picture or share a story, put your hashtags at the end of it. #hashtagsmatter #alwaysusethem #makeitconsistent.

HELPFUL HINT

IF YOU HAVE ALREADY CREATED A PROFILE OR WEBSITE, SEARCH THAT TEXT FOR KEYWORDS THAT YOU CAN USE IN FUTURE OUTREACH.

EXAMPLES OF KEYWORDS

Here are some examples of keywords and phrases used by families in their adoption outreach. Your goal is to use keywords or phrases that will encourage an expectant parent, who is looking for a family like you, to visit your website, social media account, blog or just learn more about you.

- Bilingual family
- Stay-at-home parent
- Home study approved
- Jewish family
- Same-sex couple
- Open adoption
- Closed adoption
- Adoptive parents
- Halie and Joel adopt
- Austin Texas adoption
- Christian birth mother
- Professional teacher
- Vegetarian mom
- Grill master dad

TIP SHEET

NEED SOME HELP THINKING OF KEYWORDS?
USE THIS HANDY LITTLE TIP SHEET!

Ask yourself, your friends and your family members the following questions to help you discover some keywords or phrases to use!

- HOW WOULD YOU DESCRIBE ME OR US AS A COUPLE?
- WHAT ARE MY HOBBIES AND WHAT INTERESTS ME? WHAT WOULD OTHER PEOPLE SAY ARE YOUR HOBBIES AND INTERESTS?
- WHAT DOES OUR TYPICAL WEEKEND LOOK LIKE?
- WHAT IS OUR FAVORITE WINTER ACTIVITY? FALL? SPRING? SUMMER?
- IF I PLAYED HOOKY FROM WORK, WHAT WOULD I DO?
- WHAT ARE SOME THINGS THAT ARE IMPORTANT FOR OUR CHILDREN TO LEARN FROM US?

CONTACT INFO

Setting up contact information for your adoption outreach.

ONCE YOU START YOUR OUTREACH, *you will want to make it easy for an expectant parent to reach out and contact you. It's a good idea to create new, adoption-specific contact information for use on your adoption outreach materials. It's not a good idea to share your personal contact information on anything that will be online or printed, as that opens you up to spammers, identity thieves and others who don't have your best interests at heart.*

TEXTING

We hear from our clients that most expectant parent contact comes via texting. It's important to be available via the contact methods preferred by expectant parents, and texting is it! Text messaging is not only a convenient way of connecting with a potential birth mother, it adds comfort and ease to what could be an anxiety-filled conversation. Connecting through phone calls may be overwhelming to an expectant parent. It might also be overwhelming for you as the potential adoptive parents!

Many online companies offer text numbers that direct all messages to your personal cell phone number. Google Voice is one option that is free, easy to use and can be forwarded to any number you like. Another great option is a free app called Sideline made by Pinger that creates a second number for your cell phone that you can use for calls or texting.

You can also purchase a dedicated, prepaid cell phone just for texting and communicating with expectant parents. This will add an additional layer of security when you want to prevent your personal phone number(s) from getting out to possible ID thieves.

TOLL-FREE NUMBER

KALL8 is a paid service where you can set up your own toll-free number. We recommend KALL8 for those who want an 800 number to offer to expectant parents as a way to contact you. You can visit their website at kall8.com to learn more. The cost is about $2 per month, plus calling charges should someone use your number.

Occasionally you will be assigned an 800# through one of these services that has been turned over too quickly and is still getting calls from the previous owner of the number. We suggest getting a number several weeks ahead of ordering your outreach materials so you can see if you're getting those false calls. If so, ask to be assigned a new number right away. Once you know you have a clean number, go ahead and print your outreach materials!

MARIO AND MARIA

√ Set up marioandmariaadopt@gmail.com to be used on their outreach materials, both print and online.

√ Used a service to set up a new number for texting. This number will only be used for the purpose of outreach and texting with expectant parents.

√ Purchased an 800 number for phone calls. No false calls are coming through so this number can now be put on their adoption profile and social media accounts.

HELPFUL HINT

BELIEVE IT OR NOT, TEXTING IS THE MOST COMMON FORM OF CONTACT THESE DAYS!

EMAIL ACCOUNT

It is a great idea to set up an email address that is only used for your adoption outreach. There are some great benefits to doing this including the ability to name the email something specific to your adoption outreach, for example, lucyadopts@gmail.com. This will be the address that you use on all of your outreach materials including your outreach cards, Facebook page, printed profile, website/blog, etc. Your email address should be easy to remember and hard to misspell. Don't use your last name or dates (like the year) in your email address!

NOTE: *Google's gmail allows you to add a "." to email addresses, which is a nice way to break up names like Alex. Anita.Adopt@gmail.com. The email address will work with or without the "." added!*

FOLLOW ALONG WITH OUR PUZZLE AS WE ADD THE DIFFERENT PIECES FROM EACH SECTION.

GET ALL THE WAY TO THE END TO SEE THE COMPLETE PICTURE.

SEE THE NEXT PAGE TO GET STARTED!

NOTES:

YOU'VE ADDED **FOUR PIECES!**

1 SELECT YOUR KEYWORDS
2 CREATE EMAIL ACCOUNT JUST FOR ADOPTION OUTREACH
3 SET UP TEXT & PHONE NUMBER
4 CHOOSE COVER PHOTO

ADOPTION OUTREACH IDEAS

TOPICS COVERED IN THIS SECTION:

- How to Create an Adoption Profile
- Different Ideas for Printed Outreach Materials
- A Look at Online Outreach Options
- Parent Profiles at Adoption.com
- Lots & Lots of Tips and Outreach Ideas

ADOPTION PROFILES

What are they and why are they important?

YOUR PROFILE ***is quite simply the most important part of your outreach as a hopeful adoptive parent. It must, in a matter of seconds, introduce you to expectant parents and interest them enough to learn more about you. Your goal shouldn't be to connect with each and every expectant parent but rather to connect with the right expectant parent for your family. You're aiming to create an engaging adoption profile that will make you stand out from the multitude of adoption profiles that expectant parents review.***

▲ *Your cover photo makes the first impression so make sure it's a great one!*

PHOTOS

Photos are the most important part of your profile! Many times an expectant parent will flip through your profile to get a sense of who you are without even reading your text. Your photos should be expressive, full of personality and fun, and share the activities you enjoy doing as a couple and individually. Pay close attention to photo quality since grainy, low-quality photos make it look like you don't care.

TEXT

It can be overwhelming to write the text for your profile. Make it easier by thinking of 7-9 content sections and then writing a few paragraphs for each. For some examples, look at our list on the next page. Be sure to ask your agency or attorney for their guidelines on both content and profile length.

CAPTIONS

There are times when expectant parents won't read your text (at least not at first!) so it's important for your captions to help share your story and your personality. Put as much effort into your captions as you have into selecting photos!

FUN FACTS

Just like a magazine, it can be fun to have a spot or two for fun facts or a "Top 5 list" to highlight something unique about you or to share a meaningful quote.

MEET BIG SISTER

FAVORITE SNACK: Raisins
FAVORITE PAST TIME: Dancing
FAVORITE ANIMAL: Kangaroo
FAVORITE MOVIE: Toy Story

Tatum turns three this year and cannot wait to be a big sister. She practices dressing, rocking and changing her babies. Little Bit, as we lovingly call her, is such a happy and fun loving child who is known for her big hugs and contagious smile. She loves to dance, sing, and be a helper in the kitchen. She has such a strong sense of independence and will to learn and do things herself. She likes to go to swimming and soccer lessons were she runs off her energy with all of her friends.

FUN IN FIJI

PLAYING WITH COUSINS

APPLE PICKING IN OUR COMMUNITY

TAKING CARE OF BABY

HIDE-AND-SEEK IN THE TEEPEE

FESTIVAL FOOD — YUM!

TO US, HOME IS WHEREVER OUR FAMILY IS TOGETHER

Since moving back to the states, we have renovated our house and we are putting the finishing touches on making it home. Tim has done an amazing job remodeling, painting and decorating to give it a great mix of modern and classic. Tatum loves her new space for afternoon tea with friends and teepee parties.

Living in the St. Louis area is such a great mix of large city with a small town feel. We love to support our winning Cardinals baseball and have season tickets to enjoy the games. The city has so much to offer with zoo, botanical gardens and science center which we often spend time at. When we are tired of the city, the country is just a short drive away where we go apple picking, visit the pumpkin patch, go on horse rides and are working on restoring a lake house that has been in our family for generations.

EXPLORING BEAUTIFUL FIJI

CATCHING A GAME IN ST. LOUIS

HELICOPTER RIDE!

WE ARE ACTIVE IN OUR COMMUNITY supporting a local charity which helps kids in cancer treatment. Kelly has chaired many of their events and sat on their Young Friends board. Our favorite event is Art from the Heart where the pieces from Art Therapy are auctioned off. We proudly display these in our house to remind us of our everyday blessings.

THINGS WE Love TO DO

WE LOVE TO TRAVEL, especially warm beaches. Living in Sydney for a year has given us the bug for traveling to new places and experience different cultures. When we travel, we soak up the local traditions.

WE GO TO FLORIDA every other year renting a house on Rosemary Beach. We share the vacation with our close friends and their families and spend our days at the beach and evenings by the pool BBQing.

WE LOVE TO BE ACTIVE OUTSIDE. We play at the park, go for runs and hikes, kayak and anything that gets us out of the house and in the sunshine. When it gets cold, we like to head to SkyZone and run off energy by jumping on trampolines with our friends.

WE LOVE MOVIE NIGHT AT HOME. When it is time for rest and relaxation, we snuggle up on the couch with popcorn and movie treats.

CHRISTMAS IS OUR FAVORITE HOLIDAY to celebrate family traditions. We have initiated one of Kelly's childhood traditions going to the local custard shop to pick out our fresh tree, grab some ice cream and tour the local Christmas lights. It is a great way to kick off the holiday season.

SOAKING UP THE SUN HAMILTON ISLAND

▲ *This is what it looks like when you put photos, text, captions and fun facts all together!*

PAGES (OR SECTIONS) TO INCLUDE IN YOUR PROFILE

These are just a few suggestions for the different sections of your profile. Select 7-9 for your profile and as you write your text, be sure to think about photos that relate to each section too!

- Welcome & Introduction
- About Me/Us
- Meet My Wife/Husband/Partner
- Our Kids
- Our Pets
- Where We Live
- Careers
- Our Family & Friends
- Travel & Other Adventures
- My Faith/Faith Traditions
- Traditions
- Hobbies & Interests
- Education
- Adoption in Our Lives
- Promises to Our Child
- Our Promise to You
- Closing Letter
- Contact Info/Social Media Links

HELPFUL HINT

TRY READING YOUR TEXT OUT LOUD TO HELP WITH PROOFREADING.

ADOPTION PROFILES

Selecting photos that tell your story.

YOUR PHOTOS ***and text should work together to share your story. If you don't have photos that show your particular hobby or interest, don't be shy about taking some. Photos are always looked at before text is read, so get comfortable in front of the camera! Once you have your photos gathered and text completed, think about how to present this information in a way that tells a story and appeals to an expectant parent. Here are some tips!***

▲ *A great example of a cover photo!*

▲ *Have a mix of photos by yourself and together as a couple.*

COVER PHOTO

You don't get a second chance to make a first impression, so make your cover photo a great one! Some key considerations are ensuring your face, and especially your eyes, are clearly visible- so no sunglasses, hats or strong shadows. It's important that your photo shares some of your personality, so try to be as authentic and natural as you can be.

DO:

- Use a camera, not your phone!
- Take your photo outdoors, but not in the bright sun.
- Avoid clutter in the background of your photo (like crowds or parked cars).
- Show affection!
- Consider hiring a professional photographer.

DO NOT:

- Dress in revealing or overly fussy clothing.
- Use a photo sitting at a table in a restaurant.
- Use selfies!

SUPPORTING PHOTOS

You should have several photos of you and your partner/spouse doing everyday kinds of activities. A few things to watch out for are too many pictures with sunglasses, pictures that are too light/dark or too old, showing way too much skin (no bikinis!) and any pictures with identifying information like license plates, etc. Have fun and show affection in your photos!

INDIVIDUAL PHOTOS

It's important to introduce each person individually as well as sharing who you are as a couple. Make sure to have pictures of each of you doing activities that you enjoy, both alone and with others. Highlight interesting hobbies and share what makes you tick!

A great example of how a diverse set of photos really spice up a profile!

A LIST OF TIPS

- Put it all together! Your profile should tell the story of your lives, both in text and in photos. Each page should be balanced with clear headings and a mix of photos and text.
- Make sure the text is easy to read. Small blocks of text under clear headings are easier to read or skim than whole pages of text.
- Make your profile cheery and positive. While we often come to adoption after years of loss and heartbreak, this is not the place to share those stories in detail. Many expectant parents are curious why you've chosen adoption, so be brief, positive, truthful and always share how excited you are to adopt!
- Be sure to close your profile with a warm "thank you" and encourage the reader to reach out. Of course, always include the contact information for either you or your adoption professional here too!
- Have a trusted friend or relative review your profile before it goes to print. It's amazing how a new set of eyes can pick up spelling or syntax errors. Be cautious, however, about sharing with multiple people. You know what they say about too many cooks in the kitchen! Also be aware that well-meaning friends might not understand the nuances of the adoption process, and they may offer advice that is contrary to the advice from your agency or adoption professional.
- Your agency or attorney will undoubtedly want to review your profile before you finalize, so don't forget to include them in one final review.

PROFESSIONAL ADVICE FROM

We have been working with couples and singles to create adoption profiles for over 10 years, and we love what we do! We always strive to create profiles that are creative, fun, beautiful and express our clients' unique personalities!

We have a well-organized approach to collaborating on your adoption profile and will help you with every step along the way. We work closely with your agency or attorney to ensure your profile meets their specifications as well as yours!

Not everyone wants or needs to work with a professional profile designer. For do-it-yourselfers we offer Profile Review services so you can be confident you're creating the best possible profile to use in your outreach.

We would love to help! Call us to chat about your needs, any questions or concerns and how we can help!

OURCHOSENCHILD.COM

OUTREACH CARDS

We have some ideas on the best way to use your outreach cards.

OUTREACH CARDS ***are a fantastic way to spread the word that you are adopting and interested in meeting expectant parents considering adoption. Your outreach card can catch someone's eye and provide them with a way to learn more about you, your adoption journey and how to get in touch. Outreach cards serve many purposes so let's explore a few of those here.***

Outreach cards are great to use within your social and professional circles to spread the word that you are adopting and interested in connecting with an expectant parent considering adoption. Make sure you always have outreach cards with you and share them, not only with close friends but also acquaintances from groups you might meet with infrequently like sports leagues, book clubs and school or church committees. Ask people you know to keep a card or two on-hand and share them if should they hear of an expectant parent who is considering adoption.

▲ Front and back of an Outreach Card

Outreach cards are a great tool that allows family and friends to become your "foot soldiers" on the ground, helping you with adoption outreach. You have probably been asked by several people, "Is there anything I can do to help?" and now is the time to tell them "YES! Here's how you can help!" Ask your close friends and family members to be on your "outreach team." Make sure they have outreach cards in their wallet or purse to hand out should they be in contact with someone with an unintended pregnancy who might consider adoption.

You can also share outreach cards with people in your network like your hairdresser, masseuse, dentist, doctor or your child's pediatrician. Anyone who works with the public is a key part of your outreach team—they may be in contact with a dozen people a day (or more!) and an outreach card is a great reminder of your desire to adopt and connect with an expectant parent also considering adoption.

If you are in a state that allows advertising and solicitation, then bulletin or pin-boards are a great outreach tool! These can often be found in the following places:

- Coffee shops
- Taverns
- Grocery stores
- Libraries
- College campuses
- Meeting places on campus

Lastly, don't forget the "fishbowls" retail establishments often put out for people to drop business cards into. As a bonus, you may win a free lunch!

NOTE: *Hopefully Parents does not endorse approaching an expectant mother and thrusting a card in her hand. Just because someone might look young or perhaps appears to have few resources, it's not kind to assume her baby would be better off with you. If someone is in need, then perhaps offer her the number to social services in your area or to your faith community if they work with people in crisis. These cards are intended to share your contact information with folks that are already considering adoption.*

PULL-TAB FLYERS

A great tool for outreach but how do you create one?

A PULL-TAB FLYER ***is a great tool to use to get the word out in your local community! There are lots of great places to display your flyer and, most of the time, there is no cost to post it. And of course, the more eye-catching the design, the more folks will stop and look at it. Here are some of our favorite tips to keep in mind for your flyer!***

▲ *Put a little fun and personality into your pull-tab flyer so it stands out from the crowd!*

SOME OF OUR BEST TIPS

- Make sure your contact information is clear and large enough to read in the tear-away section. The pull-tabs are not the place for fancy fonts!

- There are a few standard templates available in Microsoft Word tagged with "tear off flyer" that you can use to set up the frame of your document. When creating a new file, simply select "New From Template" and then type "tear off flyer" into the search box. Your options will pop up! There are also options available in Microsoft Publisher. Select "Flyers" and then click "others" for the tear off selections available.

- Make it fun and stand out in a positive way! We recommend staying away from the pre-made designs and/or clip art in Word or Publisher because then your flyer will look like other flyers for sales, events, etc. Use the same colors, fonts and design elements from your profile for a really custom look!

- For ideas on where you can display your flyer, look at the suggestions for Outreach Cards on the previous page. If you are ever traveling, think about taking a few with you and pinning them up at coffee shops, museums, taverns or other places you might visit.

- For more information on advertising and solicitation, please refer to pages 109-119 in this book. Hopefully Parents always recommends checking with your attorney before starting any form of advertising.

THE DESIGN OF YOUR FLYER SHOULD MATCH YOUR PROFILE FOR A CONSISTENT LOOK AND FEEL TO YOUR 'BRAND.'

OUTREACH LETTERS

Sharing your story with family and friends.

IT MIGHT SEEM ODD, ***but writing a good old-fashioned letter is a great way to reach out to a large number of people that might know of an adoption situation. You can write one letter for friends and family, those that know you really well, and another letter to send to professional contacts and acquaintances. Let's learn a bit more!***

THE PURPOSE OF A LETTER

Outreach letters serve two purposes. First, they are a good way to explain to friends and family that you are pursuing adoption. This helps keep everyone informed of your journey and limits the number of times you have to explain things to people. Secondly, an outreach letter gives a tangible way for folks to help you and get involved. You can ask people to share your letter (or outreach cards), keep their eyes and ears open for possible adoption connections and share your contact information on their social media accounts.

SOME OF OUR BEST TIPS

- When writing your letter to family and friends, use language that is conversational and casual rather than formal. A letter to family and friends is a great place to explain the process of domestic adoption and to enlist their help.

- Some folks like to include a picture of themselves with their letter. This is a nice idea when reaching out to professional contacts like doctor offices, sorority houses or youth pastors where you might not be known as well.

- Be sure to include contact information and/or outreach cards when sending your letter.

- Take your time and proofread your letter before sending it out. It is always a good idea to have someone else look it over just to be certain.

- Your letter can be mailed, emailed or a combination of both. Cast your net as far as you can!

- These are generally not considered a form of advertising. For more information on advertising, please refer to pages 109-119 in this book. We always recommend checking with your attorney before doing any sort of adoption outreach.

✓ Here is their sample letter that you can also use!

Hello,

We are hoping to adopt an infant from the United States. The current process for domestic, infant adoption is for expectant parents to select adoptive parents for their baby. We are working with an adoption agency here in town but it is also important for us to actively seek out expectant parents who may be thinking about adoption for their unborn child. YOU can be an important part of that process!

Please help us get the word out! Included with this letter are several adoption outreach cards. We would very much appreciate your help by passing these cards on to family, friends and co-workers or keeping a few in your wallet so you have them handy just in case you run into someone that might be considering making an adoption plan for their unborn baby. Perhaps you have teachers, hair stylists, dentists or coaches in your social circle. If so, please share one of our outreach cards with them too!

You can follow our adoption journey on our new Facebook page, @MarioMariaAdopt. We will be posting updates and we would appreciate your liking and sharing our page!

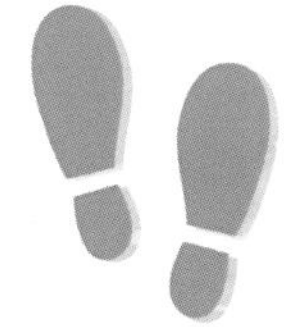

ACTUAL CLIENT STORY:
LISA & MICHAEL

OUR LETTER (BELOW) WAS VERY WELL RECEIVED. *We sent it to everyone we knew! We included outreach cards with all the letters and a magnet about our adoption to close family and friends. We had many friends tell us that they passed on our cards to pastors, hair stylists, etc. We even found many who came back and asked us for more cards. In our experience, people wanted to help but were not sure how. This was an easy way for us to spread the word far and wide.*

We did do a lot of outreach on our own (while working with an agency). It helped me (Lisa) to be doing something after the home study was complete. That time period of waiting often became very heavy and actively working on outreach helped me feel in control of something that I had no control of.

▼ LISA AND MICHAEL SENT THE FOLLOWING OUTREACH LETTER TO FAMILY AND FRIENDS

Dear Family and Friends,

If you haven't heard yet, we are hoping to adopt an infant from the United States. We are working with an Adoption Agency here in town but it is also important for us to actively seek out families who may be thinking about adoption for their unborn child.

Please help us get the word out! Included with this letter are several adoption outreach cards. Please pass them on to family, friends and co-workers. Sometimes a friend of a friend of a friend knows someone considering adoption, so even if you don't know someone directly, the people you know might know someone.

Also consider sharing our cards with your.....

- *Family doctors, Pediatricians, OB/GYN, Nurses*
- *Priests/Pastors/Youth Pastors/Rabbi*
- *Hairdressers/Nail Technicians*
- *Teachers/Child Care Providers*
- *Counselors/Social Workers*
- *Social Groups/Club Members*
- *Anyone else in your life that might be a good resource*

Thank you in advance for helping us spread the word! We are overwhelmingly excited about becoming parents to a precious child.

PRINT ADS

Exploring printed advertising.

"PRINT IS DEAD!" *is something you might hear in today's digital world but don't believe it! There are a lot of people who still get their information from print sources and advertising in print can be a valuable option in your adoption outreach plan. Believe it or not, not all areas in the United States have access to the Internet, and not everyone is online. Since print is often ignored in adoption outreach, your ad won't be one of hundreds (like on conglomerate adoption websites) but may be the only one! Let's explore some print advertising ideas!*

SOME OF OUR BEST TIPS

- Consider your local newspaper. If you live in a larger city, think about advertising in a paper that will reach smaller surrounding rural communities.

- The Penny Saver is a national publication with regional editions. These ads are inexpensive and can be quite effective! You may have other publications like this in your area such as "Buy, Sell, Trade" publications or local "weeklies."

- You can get creative and take out a billboard ad. This isn't a cheap option but it will sure draw some attention!

- Consider college newspapers, either for a school nearby or, better yet, for your alma mater!

- Your faith community might have a circular that would be a good vehicle for an ad. You can ask for the congregation's help in keeping you in prayer and connecting you to someone who may be considering adoption.

- Many neighborhoods have quarterly newsletters that can be a great source for free outreach. Any way you can expand your outreach circles is worth your time and effort!

Imagine a group of 40 adopting parents split right down the middle – 20 on each side. The group on the left signed up with an amazing agency or attorney and are currently "waiting to adopt." The group on the right side signed up with the same agency or attorney, but they're also doing their own outreach – "working to adopt" by spreading the word about their plans to adopt through personal networking and marketing.

As a group, we know the adopting parents on the right side will adopt more quickly. The alternative is impossible. Their outreach cannot negatively impact their agency or attorney's efforts – it COMPLEMENTS their efforts. That's the power of personal outreach!

Print advertising, especially in some parts of the country, is still an effective way to let potential birth parents know that you exist so they can find and learn more about you. Adoption advertising isn't about convincing someone to make an adoption plan. It's about letting those who are already considering adoption know that you're looking to adopt.

myadoptionadvisor.com/services/print-advertising

USE A FUN OR CATCHY HEADLINE TO GRAB THE ATTENTION OF READERS RIGHT AWAY.

ADVERTISING LAWS

A quick state-by-state guide to where you can or can't advertise.

THESE STATES DO NOT ALLOW ADVERTISING WITHIN THEIR BORDERS

- ALABAMA
- CALIFORNIA
- DELAWARE
- FLORIDA
- GEORGIA
- IDAHO
- INDIANA
- KENTUCKY
- LOUISIANA
- MAINE
- MASSACHUSETTS
- MONTANA
- NEBRASKA
- NEVADA
- NORTH DAKOTA
- TEXAS
- UTAH

STATES WHERE YOU CAN ADVERTISE, REGARDLESS OF WHERE YOU LIVE!

- ALASKA
- ARIZONA
- ARKANSAS
- COLORADO
- CONNECTICUT
- DISTRICT OF COLUMBIA
- HAWAII
- ILLINOIS
- IOWA
- KANSAS
- MARYLAND
- MICHIGAN
- MINNESOTA
- MISSISSIPPI
- MISSOURI
- NEW HAMPSHIRE
- NEW JERSEY
- NEW MEXICO
- NEW YORK
- NORTH CAROLINA
- OHIO
- OKLAHOMA
- OREGON
- PENNSYLVANIA
- RHODE ISLAND
- SOUTH CAROLINA
- SOUTH DAKOTA
- TENNESSEE
- VERMONT
- VIRGINIA
- WASHINGTON
- WEST VIRGINIA
- WISCONSIN
- WYOMING

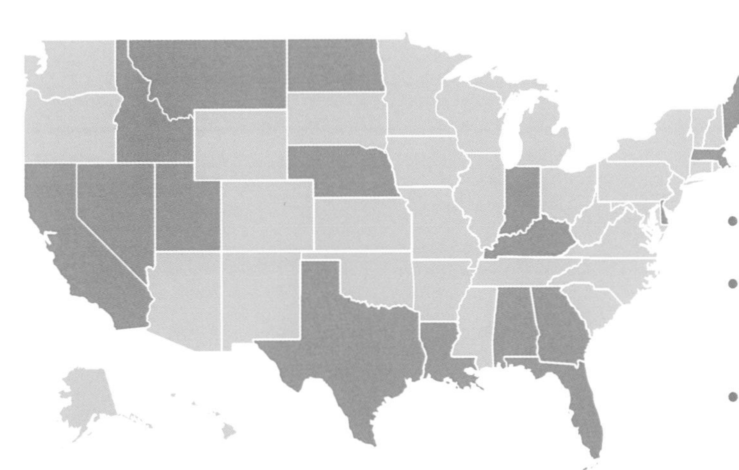

REMINDER

- Details for advertising laws by state are on pages 118-127
- You should always consult with an attorney before starting any form of advertising for your adoption outreach
- The above information comes from the following source: https://www.childwelfare.gov/topics/adoption/laws/

GENERAL OUTREACH

Creative ideas for spreading the word.

ONCE YOU HAVE YOUR OUTREACH MATERIALS, ***how do you start getting the word out? Here are some of our best ideas for creating awareness of your desire to adopt and how to start reaching out to people that might lead to a meaningful connection with an expectant parent. If you've covered the basics and want to dig a little deeper, here are some ideas for more creative outreach methods!***

- Play "Tag, You're It!" Reach out to three friends on social media and ask for their help sharing your page and your journey. When you ask a small, select group for help, people are more apt to step up and assist you!

- Consider holding an "adoption garage sale" where you solicit items from family and friends to sell at a garage sale. On the day of your sale, make large signs telling customers that all proceeds will go toward your adoption. Be sure to have copies of your profile, outreach letter and/or outreach cards available for folks to take with them. This is a GREAT time to network with lots of people, so don't sit behind the cash box; make sure you're out in the crowd talking about adoption and your outreach!

If folks know your sale is to help pursue adoption, you can generate a lot of conversation and connections! Thanks to Michelle Sarah Buie for the photo! We're so glad your yard sale was such a success!

- If you're crafty, or have crafty friends, consider a booth at a local craft fair to sell your wares. Make sure you have signs stating proceeds from your sale will go toward your adoption! Of course you will have copies of your profile and outreach cards there and make sure everyone who visits walks away with a card (and a smile!)

- Let your email do the talking! Create a custom signature for your personal email account that links back to your website, blog or social media accounts to remind people you're actively searching for a match.

- Think about friends who have small businesses and ask if they would be willing to do some cross-promotion with you. Consider friends selling products like Jamberry, Shakeology, Stella and Dot, Silpada, etc. Everyone needs help widening their audience, especially those who are marketing their businesses! Suggest a "trade" where you spend time promoting their business on your social media pages if they will share your outreach materials at their home parties or on their social media pages. ***Bonus:*** *They might consider doing a fundraiser with you with proceeds going to your adoption!*

- Don't forget grandma! If your grandma is like ours, she has a big group of friends who love nothing more than playing Bunco and talking about their kids and grandkids. Your grandma also has one mission in life: to see you happy. Let her be your eyes and ears; she will be thrilled to help and it could be an amazing connection. Sometimes you have to take a break from social media and go old-school by using the grandma network!

- Sponsor a team or event. This is a great way to get your name out there, especially if you sponsor something associated with families, babies or adoption.

> *"We created custom T-shirts for a local charity walk that we volunteered at. It was a big hit!"*
>
> ACTUAL CLIENTS, CATHERINE & WES

- Get some really fun, custom T-shirts made (or make them yourself!) and wear them when attending events with crowds such as farmers markets, community festivals, concerts, etc. Make sure to have a phone number or website listed so people can follow up if they have any questions or know of any possibilities.

- Having a blog or Facebook page can do double-duty. Along with updating people on your outreach, you can keep "How's the adoption coming?" questions to a minimum. Believe us, there will be days you don't want to ever hear that question again, so keep your network on top of your journey by updating your blog, Facebook page or other social media site regularly.

- Stay on top of social media trends. Different age groups use social media differently. If you're not on Instagram or Pinterest, you ought to be! Both are free and great ways to get your outreach materials into the media stream. **Bonus:** *You'll be the hippest parents in town once you have your own kiddo and you're already mastered Snap Chat!*

- Check with your primary care doctor, OB/GYN and even your dentist! They are on the "front lines" and often will work with patients who are in difficult situations and may be considering their options. If you have children you should talk with your children's pediatrician as well. This is a great place to leave outreach cards and/or an outreach letter!

- There's a reason politicians want you to put their bumper stickers on your car—they work! Keep your message short and sweet and be sure to include your website or text number.

- Everyday items like reusable grocery bags can be a great way to share the message that you're adopting! You can easily create and print these through websites like Zazzle.com or CafePress.com, or you can make your own with supplies easily purchased from a craft store. Make a few for family and friends too! **Bonus:** *You get to help save the planet!*

PROFESSIONAL ADVICE

Consider hosting an event that is part-social, part-fundraiser, part-outreach at your faith community or local community center. This family found great success with a "Paint Night" at their church. They raised a significance amount of money for their adoption and gained new interested followers of their journey!

HELPFUL HINT

MORE GREAT IDEAS LIKE THIS CAN BE FOUND ON OUR BRIGHT IDEAS BLOG!
HOPEFULLYPARENTS.COM/BRIGHTIDEAS

BEING ONLINE

Hopefullyparents.com personal page.

THERE IS NO DOUBT *that having a presence online is increasingly necessary in adoption outreach. It can be overwhelming trying to figure out your best options among the various platforms for getting online, so for the next few pages, let's take a look at the different options and weigh the benefits of each!*

A HOPEFULLY PARENTS WEB PAGE

A great option for being online with minimal effort is to utilize profile hosting at hopefullyparents.com. You get your own URL (web address) to give to people and you don't have to build or design anything. Your profile will be online and available for download, plus you can have an embedded video and photo galleries too.

BENEFITS:

- Minimal, one-time fee.
- Options include profile hosting, outreach cards designed to match your profile and a custom cover photo for Facebook.
- No competing with other adopting families on large adoption advertising websites. When you share a link to your page, the expectant parents see YOU and only you — there is not a mass listing of hundreds of other couples for you to compete with.

CONSIDERATIONS:

- Hopefully Parents does not advertise to expectant parents, rather it is a way for you to share your profile and contact information through your own outreach.

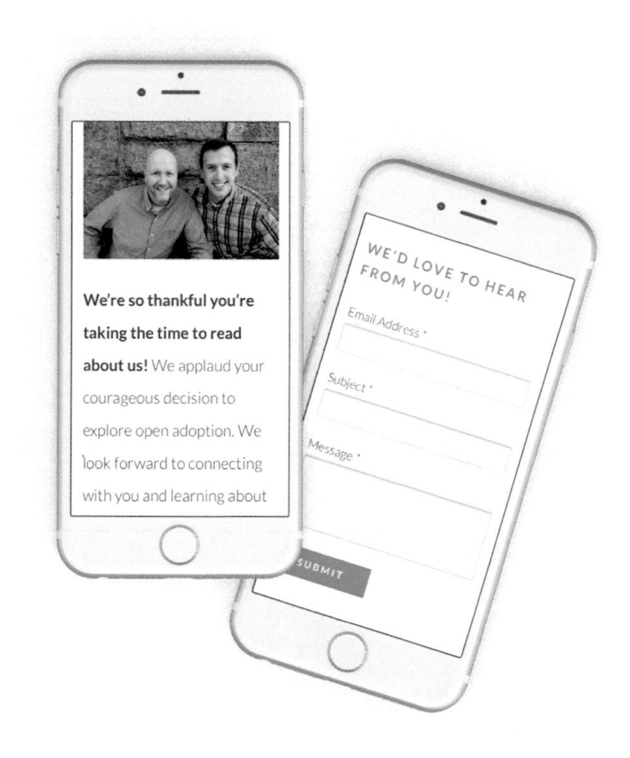

PHOTO GALLERY

If there are some favorite photos that didn't make it into your adoption profile, you can include them here in a photo gallery. Add captions and now the viewer can read to get to know you better.

VIDEO MESSAGE

Everyone likes to watch short videos, right? You can include a video message on your personal page in addition to everything else. If you want to think it over, a video can be added at a later date.

CONTACT INFO

Your contact information will be "clickable" so with one click the viewer can call, text or email you! You have lots of options to list all of the ways people can contact you.

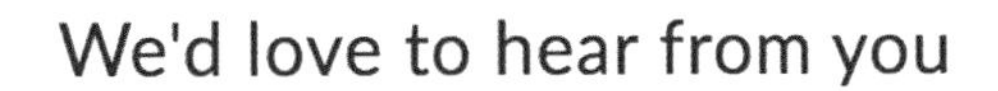

OR SEND US A MESSAGE!

SHARE YOUR PROFILE

Your profile is displayed to catch the viewer's attention, and then your entire profile is available for download so they can get to know you better!

HELPFUL HINT

PUT THE URL FOR YOUR HOPEFULLY PARENTS WEB PAGE IN YOUR EMAIL SIGNATURE.

BEING ONLINE

How to decide if a website is right for you.

OUR NEXT SUGGESTION *for getting your outreach online is to create, build and maintain a personal website. Building your own website gives you a great amount of flexibility in what to share and how you choose to share it. Just like your other outreach materials, an adoption-specific website should be branded to look like your adoption profile and other outreach tools. Is this the right option for you? Let's dive into some details that might help you decide.*

PERSONAL WEBSITE

A personal website can be a useful tool for your adoption outreach. You can have lots of bells and whistles on your site like photo galleries, slideshows, embedded videos and of course, links to your social media pages. Or it can be simple and elegant with just the copy from your adoption profile and your favorite photos.

If you're comfortable with technology, there are great sites like Wix and Squarespace to assist you in building a site without having to learn to code or use HTML. If all of that sounds daunting to do yourself, but a site sounds like a good option for you, just look in our "Additional Resources" section at the end of this book for some great options!

BENEFITS:

- It's your website and you get to control all of the content that is shown, you're not tied to a template.
- You can pack your website with keywords to encourage visitors interested in adoption.
- You have the ability to use advertising and SEO (Search Engine Optimization) to further push traffic to your site.
- You don't have to continually update it with new content, like a blog or your social media pages.

CONSIDERATIONS:

- You will need to purchase a domain name for your website and keep it active, in addition to paying for hosting for the website.
- Unless you're proficient with technology it can be time-consuming to develop your own website, and to do it well.
- You are responsible for getting traffic and attention to this site.
- A website can be expensive if you're hiring someone to build it for you.

BEING ONLINE

More ideas for your adoption website.

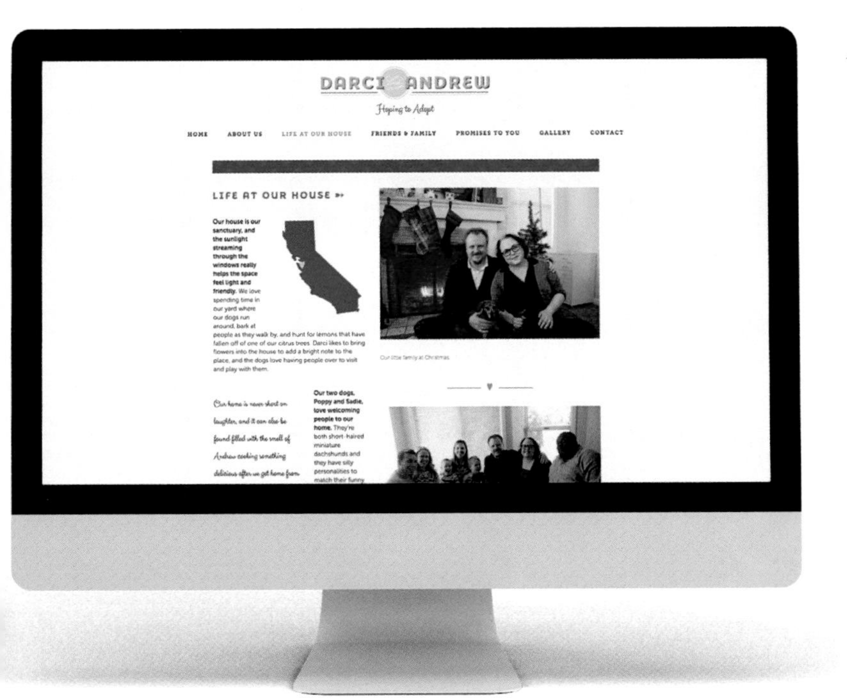

◀ MORE ROOM TO TELL YOUR STORY

When you create your own website, you can determine how many pages are included, what content is shared and what information is available. This allows you to tell your story any way you want!

You might have something really unique to share or a funny story to highlight about your life. With your own website, you can have this type of content available and easy to find. A personal website is a way to really organize your thoughts and decide how you want to "introduce" yourself to the world.

PHOTO GALLERY & VIDEOS

Having your own website means that you have the ability to show several photo galleries and/or videos. This gives your audience a chance to get to know you in specific ways. In our example here, Darci and Andrew created one gallery of their family, one of their dogs and one of just them.

If you have multiple videos, having your own site allows you to place them on your site anywhere you want. You could have a welcome video on the "Home" page, a tour of your home on a "Where We Live" page, etc. ▶

◀ DESIGNED WITH YOUR BRANDING

One of the best features of having your own website is that you can (and should!) make it look just like your profile and other outreach materials. This keeps your branding consistent and shows your audience the same message, story or feeling every time they "meet" you, which is very comforting.

If you want to be online and sign up on adoptive family websites, you must adhere to whatever standard look they are offering. But with your own website, you get to look unique and original!

BEING ONLINE

Helpful tips for setting up an Adoption.com Parent Profile

INCREASE YOUR EXPOSURE! ***Using a website like Parent Profiles is a great way to increase your exposure to expectant parents considering adoption. They work with traditional families as well as same-sex couples and single hopeful adoptive parents. They have tiered options for exposure; silver, gold, and platinum so you can choose the best option for you!***

STEP 1: PARENT PROFILES USER AGREEMENT

- Check the box "I have read and agree to Parent Profiles User Agreement."

STEP 2: GENERAL INFORMATION

- Fill out your basic information, first and last name(s).
- How did you hear about Adoption.com Parent Profiles? Select from the dropdown menu.

STEP 3: ADOPTION SERVICE PROVIDER

- Select your provider from the dropdown menu.
- Once you select your agency or attorney, they will receive an email requesting that they verify your adoption eligibility.

STEP 4: UPLOAD YOUR HOME STUDY

- To list on Adoption.com, the first and last pages of your home study are required.
- The first page should include identifying information and the last should verify that you are approved to adopt and include signature(s).

TIP: When you complete a section, hit the orange NEXT to continue on to the next step.

STEP 5: ADD PROFILE PHOTOS AND CONTACT INFORMATION

- Click "Update Profile Photo" and select your photo.

◀ TIP: Profile photo ratio is square. We recommend using a photo where your faces are centered and the focus. You'll see a circle appear over your photo. Use this tool to set a specific area to focus on.

- Click "Update Cover Photo" and select your photo.

TIP: We recommend a cover photo size of 600 pixels x 350 pixels. Keep faces in the top third and center. Avoid heads too close to the edge. Text should be right/centered and not too close to the edge.

- Hit the orange save button on both of your newly uploaded photos!
- Scroll down to fill out your contact information

STEP 6: ADD ABOUT INFORMATION

- In this section, you'll fill out your basic information, preferences for a child, work and education, and evironment.

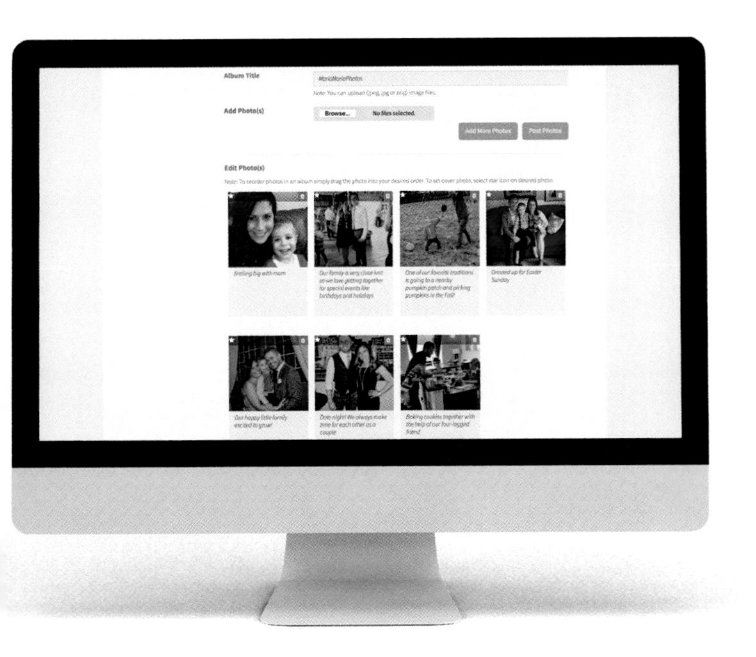

STEP 7: UPLOAD PHOTOS

- Name your album and hit browse to upload a selection of 5-7 photos.

- Edit Photo(s) by adding a caption to each. Make sure to be specific. For example, a good caption for a photo at the pumpkin patch would be, "One of our favorite traditions is going to our local pumpkin patch and picking pumpkins in the Fall!"

STEP 8: UPLOAD VIDEOS

- Uplaod your video: You can upload mp4 or mov files up to 500MB in size.

- Uplaod your video from Youtube: Search and insert your youtube video url or embed code.

- Give your video a title, example: "A Glimpse into our Life!" You can add more information with a brief description about your video. Then click "Post video."

STEP 9: LETTER

- Instructions: You are required to complete at least Section 1 or Section 2 of your letter but you have the option to complete up to 4 sections.

TIP: Your video will appear in section 1. Add a title (such as Our Family, About Us, etc.). You also have the option to add a caption to your video and write your first paragraph below that.

- You have the option of adding a highlighted quote to each section. It could be your favorite quote or an important sentence from your letter you'd like to stand out.

TIP: If you don't have a video, skip down to section 2.

- Title the section. Select a corresponding photo to upload and give it a caption! You're all set to fill in the text section.

STEP 10: ADD YOUR FAVORITES

- You can select a photo online, save to your computer and upload with a brief description

- Copy and paste a url of one of your favorite websites and then select from the photo options.

STEP 11: ADD A POST

- Think of this like a blog. Start by adding a title to your post. You can then add a photo and some brief text. You can post as frequently as you'd like. When you're done, hit post!

STEP 12: REQUEST RECOMMENDATIONS AND ENDORSEMENTS

- Endorsements: Add a quality by typing in some words that describe you, examples "Active", "Family oriented", "Fun Loving" - hit save!

- Recommendations from family and friends can give expectant parents an opportunity to see you through the eyes of others, giving them confidence that you are who you say you are. Provide their name and email and click send!

STEP 13: SOCIAL MEDIA POST

- A social media post is the text that appears with your profile when/if it is shared on any Adoption.com social media site. This is an option for Gold and Platinum Package users.

STEP 14: TEASER TEXT

- This is a line of text that appears below your profile picture for clients with the Gold and Platinum Packages. Think of it like a caption or introduction to your profile.

BEING ONLINE

Blogging is another great option for being online!

OUR LAST SUGGESTION *for getting online and sharing your adoption journey is to create and maintain a personal blog. There can be a lot of advantages to this form of outreach so let's take a closer look at the details of how to set up a blog and what the benefits are!*

▲ *This is the blog that Chris & Troy used to share glimpses into their lives and connect with new people all over the world. Read their interview on the next page!*

A blog is a useful tool for getting online in a fairly easy and inexpensive manner. A lot of people have blogs for different reasons and you might enjoy following some of them. Topics such as fashion, food, photography, running, politics and more are all discussed in blogs by everyone from professionals in their fields to stay-at-home moms.

Using a blog for adoption outreach can be an easy way to have an online presence, control the content that you want shared and create an outlet for sharing your journey with family and friends. This can be a great tool if you have the drive and ambition to learn how to set it up and make sure it stays updated with new content on a regular basis.

BENEFITS:

- There are a lot of free options to use.
- A blog gives you a place to tell stories and connect to a larger audience.
- You have an online presence that will allow anyone to see your photos and content instantly.
- It's a great way to meet new friends and join a community that understands what you're going through.

CONSIDERATIONS:

- It can be time-consuming to set up and learn if you're not comfortable with technology.
- You have to be diligent about updating your blog with new content on a regular basis.
- Unlike social media, blog posts take time. It's not 140 characters after all, a blog post is a well-written essay.
- You are responsible for driving traffic to your blog.

CHOOSING WHERE AND HOW TO BLOG

There are a few factors to consider before choosing a blogging platform. For example, is it free or do you have to pay? Another factor is how easy it is to use. Your goal in creating a blog would be to use it to share photos, stories and even videos fairly often. You don't want an exercise in frustration every time you try to update your blog or share something new.

Blogs that don't cost anything can be very user-friendly and will help guide you through the process of starting one. This is a great option for beginners who just want to share stories and boost their brand. Here are a few examples of free and easy-to-use blogs:

- blogger.com (Google)
- wix.com
- tumblr.com
- weebly.com

ADD A BLOG TO A WEBSITE

If you already own a website and want to incorporate a blog for your outreach, great! This can give you the advantage of having complete control over the look and feel of your blog. This option can sometimes require a bit more skill with design and using applications but there are usually instructions on how set this up with your website. It can even be a matter of a quick add-on within your website platform that just needs to be activated and added to your site.

GAINING MORE VIEWERS

Once you have decided on a blog and you have it set up, you will want to have people read it and share it. But how do you do that? We have a few ideas to help:

- Share your blog on social media accounts. Ask if friends and family will share on their social media too.
- Read your favorite blogs that relate to adoption. When you enjoy the post, share a comment, start a conversation and include a link back to your blog.
- When others comment on your blog, engage with them and ask them to share your blog.

BRIGHT IDEAS BLOG

Don't forget to check out the Hopefully Parents "Bright Ideas" blog on our website for things like:

- Tip of the Week
- Additional Client Stories
- In-Depth Look at New Social Media Features
- Brainstorming 101 (New Ideas)

HOPEFULLYPARENTS.COM

CLIENT INTERVIEW

An interview with clients Chris and Troy about being online.

WITH SOME INITIAL HESITATION, ***Chris and Troy decided to start a blog (and other social media accounts) to help with their adoption journey. And after a short time, they realized how valuable this outreach was and how many connections they were making. Here's some advice they have for thinking about blogging!***

WHY DID YOU START DOING YOUR OWN ADOPTION OUTREACH?

After signing with our agency, we were encouraged to do marketing and outreach on our own, as there were nearly 600 waiting families with our agency. We were hesitant at first because we are more private with personal information and family matters, but quickly realized that we needed to get the word out that we were looking to grow our family through open adoption.

WHAT DID YOU DISCOVER AS YOU BEGAN TO SHARE YOUR ADOPTION JOURNEY?

What initially started as a blog quickly grew into a Facebook page and additional social media platforms. Our hesitation to share our journey changed as we were overwhelmed with personal messages, people sharing our story and encouragement from strangers. It was then that our social media presence about our adoption journey started to take on four roles: (1) a way to keep our family and friends updated on our process, (2) a way to help others going through or planning to go through the adoption process, (3) a way to potentially reach expectant mothers and/or individuals that know of adoption situations, and (4) a way for us to stay engaged during the adoption wait.

CHRIS AND TROY CELEBRATING THEIR FIRST FAMILY CHRISTMAS WITH BABY OLIVIA

The support we have received from family, friends and even strangers during the adoption process has been so encouraging and has assured us time and time again that we made the right decision sharing our journey publicly. The process of adoption can be a roller coaster of emotions, and while most of our journey has been positive, there have been some setbacks and disappointments along the way. Sharing those ups and downs through our blog and social media outlets is a way for us to process the situations and hear from others that have gone through similar situations or who are simply keeping us in their thoughts and prayers. Our blog alone has been read by nearly 15,000 people from across the country in the last year and not once have we received anything but positivity, encouragement and well wishes from everyone that has connected with our story. It has been very moving for us and reassured our decisions and process.

SOME FIRST PHOTOS OF OLIVIA AS A NEWBORN AND A BRAND-NEW, HAPPY FAMILY!

WERE YOU CONTACTED BY ANY EXPECTANT PARENTS FROM SOCIAL MEDIA?

We connected with a number of expectant parents through email initially - them reaching out to us; however, our blog seemed to get the most traction as it was read by thousands, shared and reshared when we would post. Other connections with expectant parents took place via Facebook, text and phone conversations—we had a 1-800 number expectant parents could call. And ultimately, our first contact with our daughter's birth family was via Facebook message.

DO YOU STILL USE SOCIAL MEDIA?

Yes, we use social media to stay in contact with our daughter's birth family. Prior to our daughter being born, we created a private Facebook page and expressed to the birthparents that they could invite who they wanted to the page. We control and manage the page, but they have the ability to post as well and invite additional members on their own. We post photos, videos and updates of our daughter one to two times a week. It is super easy to keep up with, since we are typically posting to our personal social media pages, but it also gives us an opportunity to stay connected with our daughter's birth family on a consistent basis and is a platform for them to view photos, videos and updates when they want.

WHAT MESSAGE DID YOU WANT TO SHINE? The vibe and feel that we want our followers to have when viewing our social media profiles is for them to be happy and smile, to educate them on open adoption and to give them an insight into our amazing life with our daughter. We want our friends, family and people we don't know to experience the positivity of open adoption and a family that happens to have two dads.

WHAT ADVICE DO YOU HAVE FOR HOPEFUL ADOPTIVE FAMILIES?

Our biggest piece of advice for hopeful adoptive parents is to be willing to put yourself and your story out there and to maintain a positive tone to your overall journey. At first, we were very nervous with putting our story on social media, but having our blog drive our journey gave us a framework for how we told our story. We made a conscious effort to write our blog in a way that would update those close to us, but would also give expectant parents an insight into our lives. We had some ups and downs in our journey, but stayed true to our messaging and positivity. The blog posts that we received the biggest responses to were the ones that were personal, emotional, and honest. Additionally, through our blog we were asked to be guest bloggers for a number of other organizations, which increased our exposure and reach. Hopeful adoptive parents should look at the personal marketing aspect as part of the adoption journey - it keeps you engaged in the process and keeps the aspect of hope and optimism alive. You are actively being a part of the process.

▼ *Look at their great use of #hashtags!*

SEO

What is it and why does it matter?

ONCE YOU'RE ONLINE, ***it's critical to make sure people can find you! SEO is an acronym for Search Engine Optimization. We'll teach you how to harness the power of SEO to bring visitors to your site. We will help you set up your blog, website or social media accounts with embedded content that will help search engines (like Google or Bing) find your site.***

WHAT IS IT?

Search Engine Optimization (SEO) is the process of maximizing the number of visitors to a particular website by ensuring that the site appears high on the list of search results returned by a search engine.

It's not just a matter of "If you build it, they will come." Trying to maximize your site's SEO takes time and effort, but it's a critical component to your outreach.

Every Internet browser has a search engine that indexes websites and looks for keywords, content, tagged images and other clues about the information the site is sharing. This program is known as a "spider," crawling through your website (blog, Hopefully Parents page, etc.) to pick up and index all of this information. They look at the code used to create the site and pick up on repetitive language used, which can be publically visible, or words used on the back end of the site specifically for SEO and indexing. Keywords are a big part of determining whether your site is shown when someone does an Internet search.

HOW DOES IT WORK EXACTLY?

SEO starts with keywords! This is why throughout this book we have been (and will continue to be) guiding you to create content that will give you better search results and improve your chances of being found when others are doing Internet searches relevant to your adoption plans.

BRANDING + SEO

Using SEO will help your brand become more visible throughout the Internet. With a clear and consistent brand, your SEO and online efforts will be much more effective and will result in increased visibility online, meaning it will be easier for people to find you!

BE SURE ALL OF YOUR SOCIAL MEDIA ACCOUNTS AND OTHER ONLINE PRESENCE (BLOG, WEBSITE, HOPEFULLYPARENTS PAGE) ARE LINKED FOR GREATER VISIBILITY!

√ Are using their keywords on the back end of their website in the title and in the description.

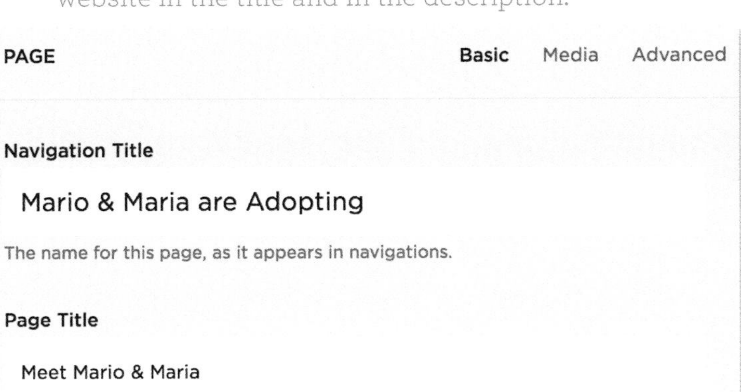

Enabled
Disabling a page is useful while it is being worked on. Disabled pages are accessible only to administrators.

Description

Hello, We are Mario & Mario from Madison, WI and we are hoping to adopt! We are very passionate about building a family through open adoption.

√ Make sure to include their keywords (using hashtags) when posting a photo on their Facebook page.

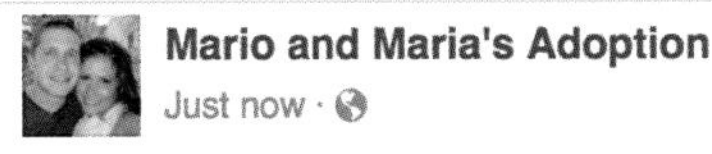

We were so lucky to spend the afternoon with our adorable new nephew!!
#marioandmariaadopt #openadoption #multiculturaladoption
#marioandmariasadoptionjourney
www.marioandmariaadopt.com

WHERE DO I USE SEO?

Now that you have a list of keywords and phrases, you want to make sure to use them! You can place them behind the scenes of your website(s) or landing pages, within your blog or use them when you are commenting on another blog. Any or all of these ideas will build your SEO.

Website/Blog:

- If you are familiar with web development or poking around in the "backend" of your website, you can easily place your keywords throughout your site where they won't be visible to a site visitor, but they will be visible to search engines. Make sure to create title tags, image tags and add meta descriptions. On the back-end of your website you should find fields for "description" or "about" where you can enter your keywords as well. Remember, when entering keywords on the back-end of a website you do not use hashtags the way you would if it were visible to the public.

Social Media:

- Use your keywords and key phrases in your adoption-specific name when you set it up, in your profile account information and especially in your posts, tweets, hashtags and images. Search engines will pick up consistent use of keywords.

TIPS TO GET STARTED

- The first 200 characters of your content are more likely to be picked up through searches, so include your keywords in places that appear first. You can even label photos or videos with keywords to aid in SEO.

- Post original content, photos and videos. Your own original content will be picked up more often than linking to content at another site.

- Posting or sharing photos or other content from sites you like is common and great for audience appeal, but make sure to use your keywords and links so it will relate back to your blog, website or social media account when someone is doing a search.

ONLINE ADS

An interview with Hal Kaufman about online advertising.

IF YOU HAVE INVESTED THE TIME AND MONEY INTO SETTING UP A BLOG, *a website or even your Hopefully Parents page, typically your goal is to gain a larger audience in order to receive more exposure. SEO is important, but it also takes a significant investment of time and effort to master. How else can you quickly increase your audience? One option is to invest in online advertising. Hal Kaufman from "My Adoption Advisor" is a nationally-known expert on adoption advertising, and he has shared some of his best-practices with us.*

WHAT IS ONLINE ADVERTISING?

There are books, courses and week long conferences on this subject. We can't cover it all, but it's important that you understand the basics because online advertising can be an effective method to reach people who are considering adoption for their baby.

In its broadest sense, online advertising encompasses any type of advertising that uses the Internet, including email marketing, display advertising, search advertising, search engine optimization (SEO), video advertising, app advertising, social media advertising, and even online classifieds. For brevity (and sanity!), we're going to focus on an effective online advertising approach for adopting parents called per-per-click, or PPC advertising.

PPC advertising is a method by which the advertiser only pays the search engine when someone clicks on the advertiser's ad, hence the name, pay-per-click. The search engine shows the ads for free based on what people are searching on and what phrases advertisers are targeting. Search engines are obviously incentivized to show only the most relevant ads to someone's search phrase because the search engines only make money when someone clicks on the ad.

WHAT'S THE DIFFERENCE BETWEEN ORGANIC SEARCH AND PAID SEARCH?

Organic or natural search results are determined by the search engine's algorithmic rankings. No one can pay the search engines for higher organic search rankings. SEO, or search engine optimization, is the practice of developing and promoting website pages in a certain way to increase the chances for the search engines to include those pages in its organic search results for specific search phrases.

Paid search results are determined by a separate algorithm. Paid search gives advertisers the opportunity to pay a search engine to have their website page displayed above or below the organic search results.

NEGATIVE KEYWORD

You don't want to waste time or money on search results that don't relate to you. It's often helpful to add negative keywords, especially if you are paying for clicks or placement. Negative keywords will exclude your site from searches for these keywords. You would list these when you set-up your ads.

Examples of Negative Keywords that should not trigger your ad:

- Pet adoption
- Cat rescue adoption
- Anti-adoption
- Adopt-a-highway
- Adopting from Africa

IT IS IMPERATIVE TO MAKE SURE ADVERTISING IS ALLOWED IN YOUR STATE BEFORE YOU BEGIN YOUR OUTREACH!

Google parents looking to adopt a newborn

All Shopping Videos News Images More Settings Tools

About 624,000 results (0.99 seconds)

You Are Not "Giving Up" - You Are Choosing Life For Baby
Ad www.americanadoptions.com/ (800) 236-7846
Call 24/7 for Free Adoption Info. Get Started Now - 1-800-ADOPTION.
Free 24/7 Counseling · Find your perfect family · No obligation
Services: 24x7 Specialist Support, Legal & Medical Advice, Living Expense Assistance

Newborn Baby Adoption - Most Affordable Adoption Programs
Ad www.angeladoptioninc.com/Adopt-Newborn
Start Your Journey & Apply Today!
Over 1,000 Adoptions · Free Application · Personalized Services · Caring Staff · A+ BBB Rating
Adoption Costs · Free Application · Frequent Questions · The Adoption Process · Success Stories

Pregnant & Choosing Adoption? - Find A Family For Your Baby.
Ad adoptionconnection.org/
Open Adoption Means You Choose The Family And Remain In Your Baby's Life.

Adoption: Children's Program - Dir. & Computer Exec yearn to
Ad www.jodi-and-mark-adoption.com/
adopt 1st baby. Pls call if you are giving up a baby for adoption. Expenses Paid

Adoption Profiles Helping Hopeful Parents Adopt a Baby
https://www.adoptimist.com/
Adoptimist is the leading adoption website, connecting expectant mothers with ... Adoptimist Connects Pregnant Women with Adoptive Parents Looking To Adopt.

Adoption Situations - Birthparents Seeking Adoptive Families
https://lifetimeadoption.com/adoptive-families/birthparents-seeking-families/
This birth mom is looking for a stable Christian family. Either a happily married couple or a single parent is ok for her baby. She is not looking for any assistance ...

Adoption Profiles of Waiting Families Looking to Adopt a Child
www.friendsinadoption.org/potential-adoptive-families/
Read adoption profiles of potential adoptive families looking to adopt a child. All families legally approved to adopt in the United States. 1-800-98-ADOPT.

Birth Mother Seeking Adoptive Parents For My Baby | Adoption Network
https://adoptionnetwork.com/waiting-families
If you are a Birth Mothers seeking adoptive parents, ANLC is here to help! We have adoptive families who can help you with pregnancy-related expenses.

PAID ADVERTISING

These sponsored ads are boosted in the search results and drive traffic to your website or social media account. They use 'pay-per-click' which means you pay every time your ad is clicked on.

ORGANIC SEARCH

These search results displayed are based on the most relevant content that Google matches from their index to your search.

PROFESSIONAL ADVICE FROM

My name is Hal Kaufman and I created My Adoption Advisor in 2008 with a clear Mission: to help families connect with the right birth parents more quickly and safely. Through our training and consulting programs we are accomplishing our goals, as well as helping you reach yours.

My wife and I adopted our two sons in 2005 and 2007. We adopted them both domestically and brought them home from the hospital just a few days after they were born.

DURING THE LAST SEVERAL YEARS we've developed well over 100 adoption websites and advertising campaigns for adopting parents and have been the steward of more than $275,000 in PPC spending. Call us today to learn more about the intricacies and benefits of online advertising!

My Adoption Advisor

Bonus Coupon Code:
ESSENTIAL50

If you apply this code to your purchase of our Adoption Advertising & Networking Course, you'll receive a 50% discount. As an added bonus, your purchase receipt will contain a 10% coupon code for use on any subsequent purchase of any of our services.

www.myadoptionadvisor.com

ONLINE ADS

How to set up and utilize advertising online.

GOOGLE ADWORDS ***offers several options for paid advertising and depending on your goals, some might be a better use of your dollars than others. For instance, do you just want to get as many people as possible to see a link to your blog in their search results? Do you want to really target a specific audience with a graphic that links to your adoption website? Let's look at some more options for online advertising!***

WHAT IS GOOGLE ADWORDS?

AdWords is Google's paid advertising platform. All sizes of companies, non-profit organizations and individuals, including adopting parents, use AdWords to connect with people they're trying to reach. The AdWords platform encompasses many types of paid advertising, but we'll continue to focus on PPC advertising because it's the most efficient and cost-effective type of advertising for adoptive parents.

With PPC advertising, Google operates a real-time auction each time someone performs a search on its network. If an expectant parent searches using "I'm considering adoption for my baby," for example, Google instantaneously analyzes its AdWords advertisers who have a keyword phrase related to the search phrase. Through its proprietary algorithm, it determines which of the advertisers' ads it's going to display to the searcher, and in what order it's going to display them. The ads that show up on a page represent the "winners" of the auction. The ads appear above and below the organic, or natural, search results.

WHAT IS NEEDED TO CREATE AN ADWORDS CAMPAIGN?

When someone clicks an online ad, they're redirected to a website. Therefore, before you create an online advertising campaign, you must have an adoption website. While many people pay for a listing on adoption advertising websites like Adoptimist or Parent Profiles, you don't want to invest your money in a campaign that drives traffic to those websites because you would be benefiting the listing company and the other adopting parents.

Instead, create your own adoption website or host your profile on HopefullyParents.com. Only then will every dollar you invest go toward helping a potential birth parent learn about you (and only you!)

After you have a website, you need to consider the following options when you begin an AdWords campaign:

- Location: Location targeting gives you control over whether your ads are shown to people in a geographic location. Adopting parents may target the United States but exclude states that prohibit advertising so their ads won't display in those states.

  NOTE! *See page 29 for a list of states where advertising is illegal.*

- Language: To decide when to show your ads, AdWords compares your Language setting to a searcher's Google language setting or the language of the searcher's search query.

KEEP CAREFUL NOTES ABOUT HOW YOUR ADS ARE PERFORMING BEFORE INVESTING LARGE AMOUNTS INTO ADVERTISING.

- Budget: The daily budget is the amount you are willing to invest in click costs each day. For example, let's say you wanted to invest in a daily budget of $10 and you wanted to run your ad for one month, with a maximum amount spent of $300. Google can exceed this $10 daily budget by up to 20% on any given day, but during the whole month your ad runs, Google will stay within your $300 maximum. Each day begins with a fresh daily budget, regardless of what occurred during previous days. Under spent dollars one day are not carried forward to the next day, meaning if on Friday you spent $8.00, on Saturday Google would not charge you $12 to balance it out.

- Keyword: Google compares your keyword or keyword phrases to each search phrase to determine whether it may be appropriate to show your ads to the searcher.

- Bid: A bid is the maximum amount you are willing to pay for a click on your ad.

- Ad Copy: This is your ad text. It includes two, 30-character headlines, an 80-character description, and a URL or website address where Google sends the searcher to after he or she clicks on the ad.

There are several keyword match types (e.g., broad phrase and exact match), negative keywords and other elements that give advertisers greater control over their campaign. Large campaigns could have hundreds of ads and thousands of keywords, among other complexities.

In poker, there's a popular saying that the game takes 5 minutes to learn and a lifetime to master. Advertising with AdWords is similar. As you can infer from the list of required elements (location, language, etc.), it is deceptively simple to create an AdWords campaign. However, optimizing the campaign to maximize the relevant traffic you can bring to your website while minimizing the cost for that traffic is both an art and a science.

WHY USE GOOGLE ADWORDS?

- Google is the biggest and most popular search engine on the Internet today.
- It increases the potential number of connections made through common interests through the use of keywords.
- It is already linked to your existing Google email account. (If you don't have one, it is simple to set one up!)
- You are able to set a budget for each ad campaign and you are able to modify that budget in response to ad performance.
- You have the opportunity to run multiple ads at once and test which one is more successful.
- You can determine the states and regions were you want your ads to run. Be sure to check with your attorney so you know which states are legal to advertise in and which are not.
- Using Google AdWords' analytics, you will be able to see how many people click on your ad, where they are from, what device they use to view your ad and what they did after viewing your ad. You can use this data to fine-tune your ads to maximize your impact.

CREATING VIDEOS

Why use videos in your adoption outreach?

WE HAVE ALL HEARD OF VIRAL *videos creating an instant viewing sensation on the Internet. It seems like people are sharing and buzzing over a new video every week. Your goal doesn't need to be to create the next big viral video, but rather to create a video that is fun to watch and shares something essential about you to expectant parents. The following has been provided by Tim Elder, proud dad of two (through infant adoption and Founder of InfantAdoptionGuide.com and AdoptionProfileVideo.com.*

THE BEST TOOL IN YOUR TOOLBOX

Your adoption profile is the most important part of the domestic adoption process because it is how expectant parents will get to know you. Adoption profile videos will take your profile and your outreach efforts to the next level. Why? Here are 3 BIG reasons:

1. SHOW & TELL

Through video, you can SHOW expectant mothers what your life is like and what kind of life their child will have in your family. You also TELL your unique story by talking directly to her, showing your sincerity and your emotion.

2. CONVENIENCE

Videos are easier to watch than at any time in history. You can watch wherever and whenever you want - on a smartphone, tablet or computer. This convenience makes connecting with expectant mothers even faster.

3. STAND OUT FROM THE CROWD

There are thousands of families looking to adopt, but few take the time to create an amazing video. Your video will stand out from the crowd because an expectant mother can see your face and hear your voice. This can result in you being chosen MUCH faster than other families.

This may seem obvious, but not all profile videos are created equal. In fact, not all profile videos are even good.

COMMON MISTAKES

Here are a few things to avoid when creating your video:

- Your "video" is only a photo slideshow set to music. Communicating directly with an expectant mother through the camera is so much better because it allows you to connect with her.
- You don't plan out your video (figure out what to say, where to record, etc.) before you start filming.
- Your profile video is way too long. Ideally, it should be three minutes or less.

Don't just sit on the sideline—get started making your adoption profile video today!

PROFESSIONAL ADVICE
ADOPTIONPROFILEVIDEO.COM

If you want to learn more than the information I shared here, I have a special online training program that will help you. It's called Adoption Profile Videos Made Easy!

I hold your hand as we walk through how to create and share a special profile video that will touch the heart of an expectant mother, so you connect with her faster and reach the dream of building your family through adoption.

Get started at AdoptionProfileVideo.com. I'll see you there!

VIDEO TIPS

Some ideas on making interesting videos.

YOU'RE READY TO GO FOR IT *and create your own video, hooray! The last thing you want to do is spend a lot of time talking to the camera, posting a video online and not getting any attention from it. Therefore, we have put together a list of tips to consider before and after you make your video to make sure it is ready for public viewing and will get the attention that you are hoping for. Check them out below!*

- When creating a video, have fun and loosen up! People can always tell when you are uncomfortable and not being yourself. Laughter speaks louder than words!
- Sharing multiple videos of you side by side and talking to the camera is boring! It won't hold anyone's attention, let alone help the audience engage or connect with you. Make your video more interesting by showing the activities you enjoy doing together and then add audio of you chatting about your hobbies and interests.
- Add text captions to explain the video in better detail. Be sure to use your keywords and link back to all of your social media accounts and websites.
- Choose fun topics that you are interested in that showcase who you are, such as "How To" videos of you planting in the garden, making a craft, creating a DIY project for the nursery, baking your favorite cookies, fixing something in the garage, etc.
- Start with a clear action statement introducing the video to let your audience know what they are about to see. Something like "We are making the BEST chocolate fudge cookies in the entire world! This is how our family loves spending free time together!"
- Close with a great caption that encourages the viewer to take action. For example: "For more information on Greg & Stacy's Adoption Journey, check out our website www.namehere.com" or "Visit ClairesAdopting.com to learn more about me!"
- Three minutes goes quickly! Plan ahead to make sure your video is no longer than three minutes or you will risk the viewer clicking away before seeing your contact information.
- Once you've created your video you will need to host it online. Common third-party hosting platforms are YouTube, Vimeo, or Wistia. Each will have a user-friendly process to upload your video and to add your keywords, title and other information. Once your video has been uploaded you will be able to generate a URL or link for your video so you can share your video with others! Be sure to add your link to your social media accounts and embed it on your website.
- After sharing your video on social media, you will want to make sure to title and link your video. Tag your friends involved, add a detailed description using your keywords and link your video to your website and all your other social media accounts.

GO TO VIMEO.COM AND VISIT THEIR 'VIDEO SCHOOL' PAGE FOR HELP ON CREATING VIDEOS.

VLOG & YOUTUBE

An interview with 'Bits of Paradis' family.

THE FOLLOWING INFORMATION ***is from our interview with Brittany Paradis. Brittany started a YouTube channel "Bits of Paradis" and now has a following of over 150,000. Brittany and her husband, Joe, documented their adoption process (and now, life with a baby) through videos and in this interview they share helpful suggestions for those considering vlogging! (aka video-blogging!)***

Bits of Paradis

BRITTANY PARADIS... ... ALL THE LITTLE BITS OF ME

WHY DID YOU CHOOSE YOUTUBE TO HOST YOUR VIDEOS?

In 2014, we started our YouTube channel "Bits of Paradis" in hopes of sharing our fertility journey/adoption process with others. Once we chose to start our family through adoption, we were excited to use this platform to reach out to potential birth parents. YouTube is an easy and user-friendly platform to host videos, and it makes it effortless for people all over the world to share them.

WHAT WOULD YOU SAY TO SOMEONE CONSIDERING VLOGGING FOR THEIR OUTREACH?

Pictures are great, but they can also be a little generic and out of context. When we started our adoption process, we looked at other adoption profiles to give us a better idea of how to put our profile together. It was interesting how all of the profiles started to blend together after reading through just a few. I'd imagine birth parents feel the same way when they are searching through profile after profile. They were all different, but very similar at the same time. It was hard to get a true sense of who the couple was, even after reading through their descriptions.

Including a video with your profile allows for a more intimate and candid look into who you are, what your relationship looks like, and the true emotions behind what you're relaying to potential birth parents.

JOE AND BRITTANY HOLDING THEIR BEAUTIFUL BABY GIRL, HARPER

Aside from that, I'm sure birth parents appreciate the convenience of being able to watch a video of a couple, no matter how short or informal. It's a nice change of pace from having to read through an entire profile to get to know them. Even just adding in some clips of home videos, along with your pictures, can go a long way in helping birth parents feel a connection with you. If you'd like to take it a step further, you can do an interview–style video with home videos throughout. Just remember to be yourself, and don't afraid to be genuine and raw.

WHAT WAS THE MAIN THING YOU WANTED TO SHARE THROUGH YOUR VIDEOS?

Expectant parents have such an overwhelming decision ahead of them, and we couldn't imagine how difficult it would be to choose a couple to raise a baby. We wanted to show them how much we loved and cared for them already, and who the couple behind the picture was. We wanted to give them a true and raw look into our struggles of trying to become parents, and how excited and hopeful we were to become a family through adoption.

DID YOU WRITE OUT A SCRIPT OR JUST TALK FOR YOUR VIDEOS?

We liked talking throughout the video. Almost like we were sitting across the table from potential birth parents, having an open and candid conversation with them. We thought the birth parents might also like the convenience of watching a video to get to know us, instead of having yet another adoption profile to read through. You can also get a better sense of the emotions behind what a person is saying by listening to them tell a story, versus just reading it. This alone can help birth parents start to form a real connection with you.

WHAT MESSAGE DID YOU WANT TO SHINE?

Our theme was, "This is who we are." We had faith that by being genuine and our true selves, prospective birth parents would feel it was "the right fit" if it was meant to be.

THE TECHNICAL DETAILS

We utilized Final Cut Pro on our MacBook Pro laptop to edit the videos. However, there is a large amount of free movie editing software out there. It can take some time to learn how to use these programs, but they're usually pretty self explanatory, and are easy to pick up, if you put the time in. We shoot our videos home movie style, and simply set up our camera on a tripod for the sit down interview portions. We also know a few couples that hired videographers to come take home videos of them in their home or at the park. You can even hire a video editor to put your video together if you'd like. We personally feel any video is a good video. Whether it's just a raw, unedited home video, or more of a production like we previously mentioned. Decide what kind of feeling you want your video to have, choose what message you want to have come across, and create a video that allows your personality and creativity to shine through. Just like you would do with your adoption profile. Remember to just be you.

Meeting with potential birth parents can be such a scary and intimidating experience. Our advice to adoptive couples is to always just be yourself. It makes the process so much easier in the long run. You always want to ensure that you represent your true selves through the entire adoption process from start to finish. If birth parents choose you because of your video, they are expecting that version of you moving forward. That is why it is essential to be genuine at all times.

Popular uploads

Adoption Birth Vlog | Our Adoption Journey
5 months ago • 169,384 views
We are so grateful for the miracle of adoption, and that through it, we were able to have a family. We hope yo...

SAT VLOGGING | House Tour!!
1 year ago • 141,708 views
I was feeling a bit under the weather this Saturday, so I decided to do a HOUSE TOUR for this Saturday's vlog...

First 48 Hours at Home with a Newborn! | BITS OF PARADIS
5 months ago • 82,968 views
Joe and I brought our little baby girl home from the hospital! A moment we've always dreamed of. See ...

FALL HOUSE TOUR | Saturday Vlogging
3 months ago • 60,790 views
Come decorate for fall with me!

Q&A With Our BIRTH MOM! | Open Adoption | Bits of Paradis
4 weeks ago • 58,882 views
I sat down with our Birth Mom to answer some of your most asked questions: ...

SURPRISE ADOPTION ANNOUNCEMENT | A Special Shopping Trip
9 months ago • 55,570 views
Adoption pregnancy announcement! Joe and I have been chosen by birth parents! Join us on a special ...

▲ *A sampling of the videos you can find on Brittany & Joe's channel. To view, search for "Bits of Paradis" on YouTube.*

NOTES:

TRACK YOUR PROGRESS WITH OUR PUZZLE MAP!

YOU'VE ADDED SIX PIECES!

1 CREATE ADOPTION PROFILE 2 GET OUTREACH CARDS 3 WRITE LETTERS & PULL-TAB FLYERS 4 GET ONLINE 5 SET UP SEO 6 MAKE OUTREACH VIDEO

SOCIAL MEDIA

TOPICS COVERED IN THIS SECTION:

- How to Set Up a Facebook Community Page
- Options for Paid Advertising within Facebook
- How to Set Up Accounts with Twitter, Instagram, Pinterest and YouTube
- Tips for Using Social Media for Adoption Outreach

SOCIAL MEDIA

Why it matters for adoption outreach.

ADOPTION IS FOREVER CHANGED ***by the world of social media. Now more than ever, people are making meaningful connections via the use of social media. Utilizing social media for adoption outreach may be time-consuming, especially if you use multiple applications, but it is vital to your adoption outreach to jump in! Using social media effectively is a powerful way to quickly expand your networking circles.***

GETTING STARTED WITH SOCIAL MEDIA

Social media platforms such as Facebook, Twitter and Instagram each serve a unique purpose, and each can benefit your outreach in different ways. It is important to master one application and get comfortable using it before moving on to others. You might already be using Facebook and Instagram in your personal life and that's great! This next section will show you how to set up an account and best use each platform as it relates to adoption outreach.

PLATFORMS DISCUSSED:

- Facebook
- Twitter
- Instagram
- Pinterest
- YouTube/Vlogging

Social media can be used as your primary online presence, or it can be a continuation of an online presence you've already established through blogging, a website or even a YouTube channel. As you build your online presence remember to keep account names, photos and hashtags consistent across all platforms. It's also critical to link all of your accounts. A visitor should be able to easily jump from your blog to your Facebook page and back again.

The content you share or curate can be the same or different on each social media platform. Some people like to post the same story or message to all of their social media accounts each time. If they share a story about an ice cream cone, you will see that story on Facebook, Instagram, their blog and Twitter. Other people like to have a variety, so if you see a story on Facebook and click over to their blog, a different story will appear. How often you post and how comfortable you are with each platform will likely determine which strategy is best for you.

MARIO AND MARIA

√ Follow along as Mario and Maria set up an account with Facebook, Instagram, Twitter and Pinterest.

√ Mario and Maria are using the same cover picture for all accounts to keep the consistency.

√ They are using the name "MarioandMariaAdopt" for all of their social media accounts.

THE USERNAME YOU CHOOSE FOR YOUR SOCIAL MEDIA ACCOUNTS SHOULD RELATE TO ADOPTION IN SOME WAY.

STARTING WITH FACEBOOK

Let's start by looking into the many layers of Facebook because when it comes to sharing content and connecting with other people, Facebook is king. Right now, there is not a better social media platform for adoption outreach than Facebook. We will go into detail on how best to utilize Facebook for your outreach by setting up a community page, suggesting what kinds of content to share on that page and different options you have for paid advertising. There is a lot to cover, so let's get started!

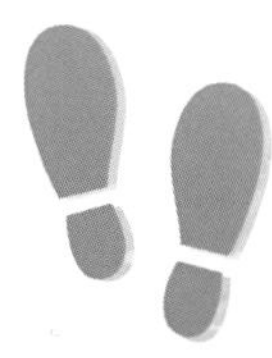

ACTUAL CLIENT STORY:
BRITTANY & BARRY

▲ Brittany and Barry share lots of love with their large family of 11 kids!

I think social media has made a tremendous difference in the adoption world. Social media allows for outreach in ways which never existed 20 years ago. It has expanded the search boundaries for agencies to be endless. Little ones who are much more difficult to place because of special needs, are finding forever families. Older children are finding families. Multiple and sibling groups are staying together and finding families as well. Hopefully, the outreach will only grow exponentially and allow more and more children to find their forever families and decrease the numbers of children stuck in the system.

When we first began our adoption journey 11 years ago, most of the outreach was through word of mouth. It was through church or social groups and friends or family. We have adopted 9 children in the last 11 years and the majority of our matches have been made with the assistance of social media.

Another way social media has changed adoption is that it facilitates the nurturing of relationships within the triad. We have contact with all our birth families using email, Twitter, Facebook, Snapchat and/or Instagram. I can send a picture of my son to his birth mom with peanut butter in his hair and then 15 minutes later I can catch a video of him singing a song to his dog. It's the little moments, that I'm willing (and wanting) to share, which have built the relationships that my children have with their birth families. It's those little moments that are so tough to lovingly convey in a letter to an agency every six months because they happen so frequently. Social media has fostered a love, a respect and a trust between us in that it has enabled us all to easily share the love we all have for our little one.

FACEBOOK

Creating a community page for your adoption outreach.

A COMMUNITY PAGE ***is the best way to use Facebook for your adoption outreach. Your Facebook community page will be a public page where you can post updates, get friends and family members involved and share your search with a large network of people. Getting lots of people to look at your page will increase your chances of being connected to expectant parents considering adoption. In the following section, we will walk you step-by-step through the process of setting up a Facebook community page and teach you how to use it for outreach!***

Your community page will be nested within your current, personal Facebook account. If you don't have a Facebook account yet no worries! Just go to Facebook.com and click on "Create" on the top blue banner, next to "Home". If you do have an account just sign in and then start by selecting “Create a Page” from your home page or news feed in Facebook. That will bring you to a page that looks like the example below. Select the “Community or Public Figure” icon. In the section below we outline some of the reasons why using a Community Page, rather than a Personal Page, is important.

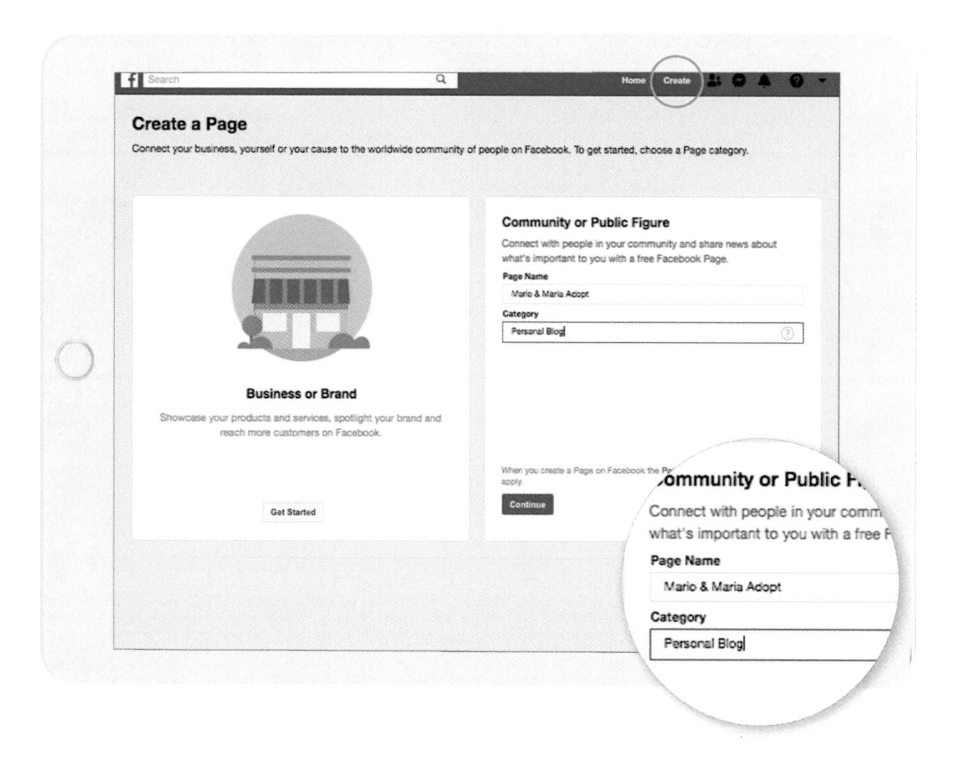

From this pop-up, fill in the name of your page. It could be something like “Jack and Jill Adopt” or “Lucy and Ethel Hope to Adopt.” Be sure your page name clearly shares that you are hoping to adopt. Type "Personal Blog" into the category section. When you’re done, click the 'Continue' button to start setting up your page.

NOTE: *Someone viewing your adoption-specific community page cannot find your personal page or the personal contact information you may have used in setting up your personal page. They are not linked in any way visible to the public.*

WHY USE A COMMUNITY PAGE?

- You will be able to tag your friends as well as other business or community pages.
- Your personal Facebook page remains private, but you can easily leverage your current friends by inviting them to follow your new page.
- You can select a target audience and use your keywords as well as SEO to further promote your page.
- A community page will allow others to “share” your page to help with gaining a larger audience. This is not an option with a regular Facebook profile.
- People can "like" your community page, whereas with a personal page people would have to send you a friend request.

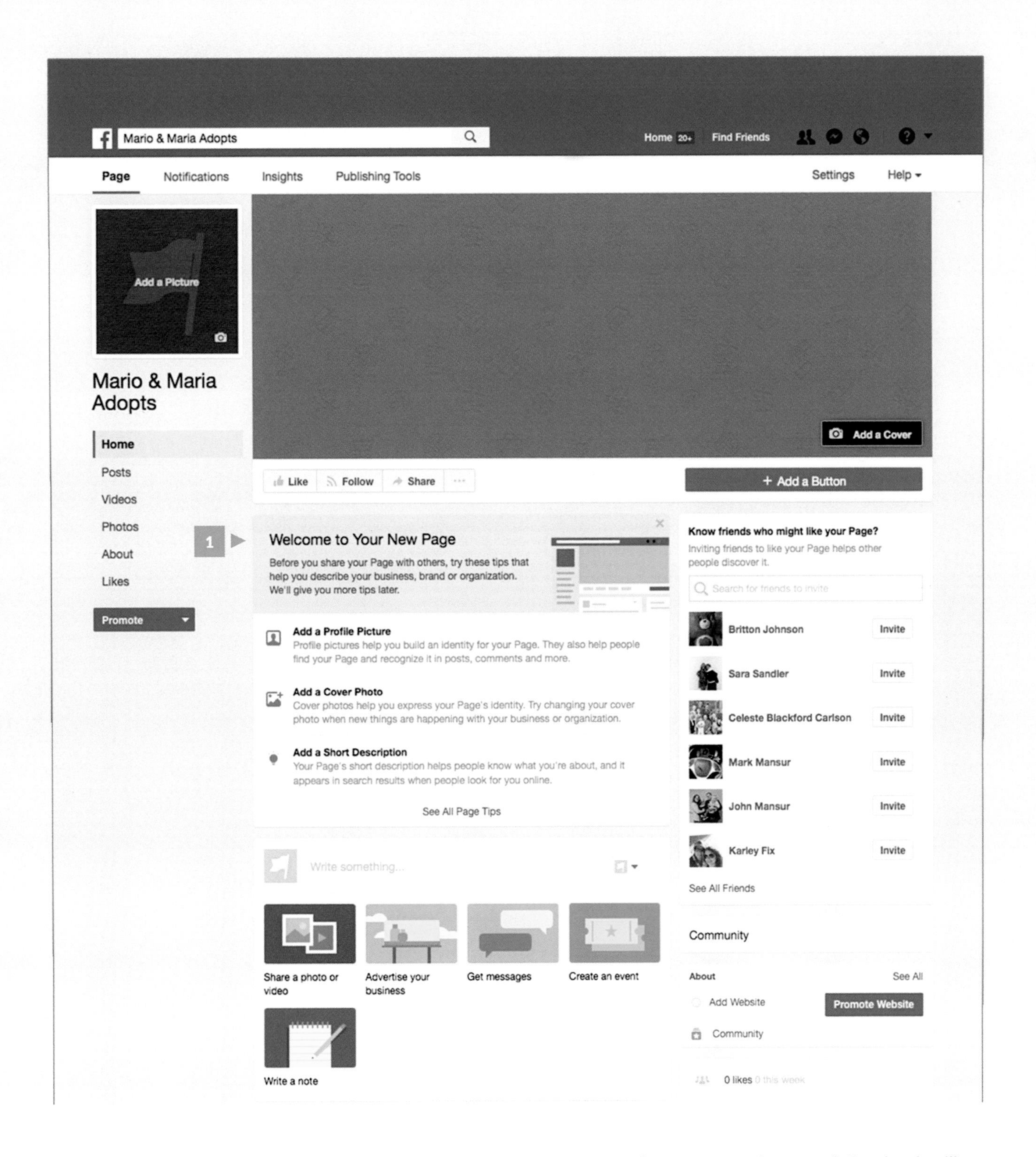

1. WELCOME Now that your page is created, Facebook will walk you through the steps needed to complete the setup of your page. As you explore this page, you will also find Page Tips that can help you, handy tracking tools, the ability to invite your friends to this page and more. We will cover these items in more detail in the following pages!

FACEBOOK

Completing your adoption outreach page.

NOW THAT YOUR PAGE IS CREATED, ***it's time to set up all of the details! In this section we will help you understand what information is important to share and how to enter it properly. Most importantly, once you have your page complete, you can start sharing it with friends to gain an audience to help you in your adoption outreach.***

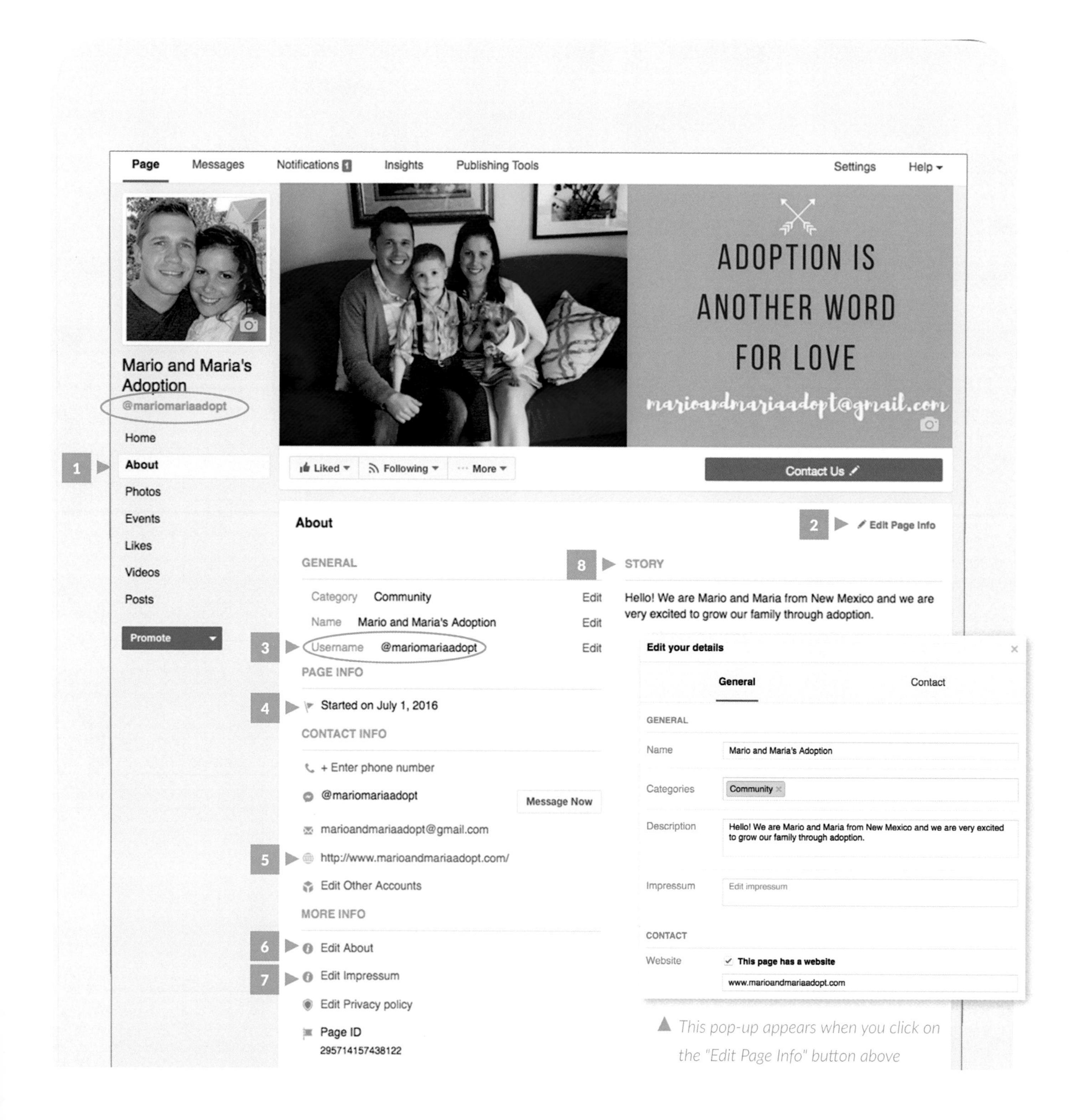

▲ *This pop-up appears when you click on the "Edit Page Info" button above*

1. ABOUT The "About" tab is where you'll enter or edit the essential elements of your page. These items are visible to the public, so don't enter personal information.

2. EDIT PAGE INFO When you click on the "Edit Page Info" icon, a pop-up window will appear (pictured on page 56) for you to make changes to your page information. These might have been filled in when you set up your page but if not, or if you want to make changes, this is where you can make any edits.

3. USERNAME This is REALLY IMPORTANT! There are several spots to create a username for your page. This creates the unique URL, such as facebook.com/ClairesAdoption. Facebook will only allow you to add this ONE TIME so be very careful to choose wisely and check for spelling. You will see two different spots circled on the picture to the left. These are just two different places to accomplish the same thing. It doesn't matter which you use.

4. START DATE The date your adoption journey began or the date you set up your page.

5. WEBSITE List your blog, website or Hopefully Parents page.

6. ABOUT - SHORT DESCRIPTION The "About" section is visible to the public and is a great place to share a few sentence about you, your journey and your desire to adopt. This text is also picked up by Facebook and is used to "suggest" your page to viewers looking at adoption-related pages. You can also add your home study status and the name of the agency or attorney you are working with.

7. IMPRESSUM This is your standpoint from a legal perspective. You can either leave it blank or write something like "Jack and Jill comply with the adoption laws of Texas."

8. STORY - LONG DESCRIPTION This can be a longer story about your adoption journey and why you created this page. The content in this area will display when someone views the "About" tab on your page. This section can be up to 2,000 words long and should contain your contact information, your other social media accounts or website URL, your agency name and any other content you would like someone to know. Be sure to be detailed and use keywords and phrases since words used here will help filter search results and your target audience.

HELPFUL HINT

ONCE YOUR PAGE IS CREATED, YOU CAN TOGGLE BETWEEN YOUR PERSONAL ACCOUNT AND YOUR NEW ADOPTION OUTREACH PAGE EASILY FROM THE TOP RIGHT DROP-DOWN MENU ON ANY FACEBOOK PAGE.

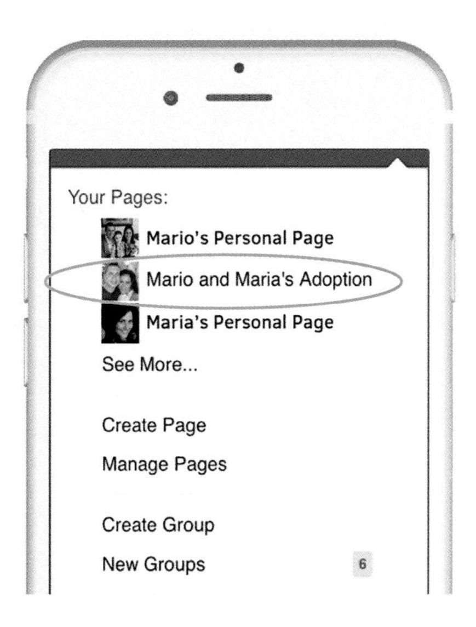

FACEBOOK

Setting up your profile and cover photos.

IT'S TIME TO GET PERSONAL, *and that means turning a common, every day community page into your page! The best way to do that is to add your profile and cover photos. This gives your page an identity and something for people to connect with. There is actually some strategy behind choosing your profile and cover photos, so let's take a look at how you can use these spots for maximum effect!*

1. PROFILE PHOTO The profile picture is smaller in size on your page but it's the first thing that anyone will see when searching for or landing on your page. That's why this photo is so important! If you haven't already selected a profile photo, take some time and pick the right one. For some help, use the same guidelines for choosing a cover photo on your adoption profile, as outlined on page 20.
2. COVER PHOTO The cover photo is larger and offers a chance to give your page some personality! This is where you can get creative and show the purpose of this specific page, almost like a title. It's important to share that you are hoping to adopt, include your names and perhaps another photo, a short quote or contact information. On the next page, we will show a few options for creating fun cover photos to make your page stand out from the crowd!

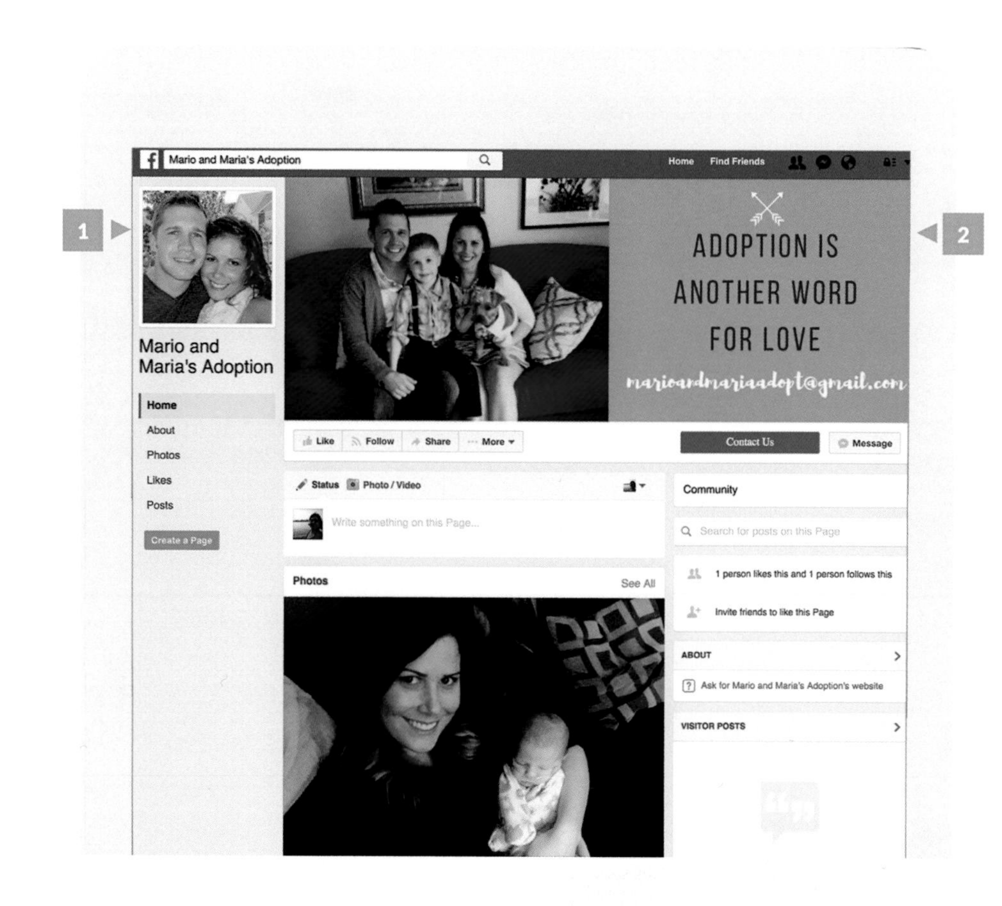

Keep in mind that when your Facebook page is viewed from a smartphone, the cover photo will get cut-off and only the middle 65% will be shown. Watch where you put vital information and make sure any pictures aren't being cut-off in an awkward place. After you upload your cover photo, make sure to log into Facebook from your phone and ensure your cover photo still looks good.

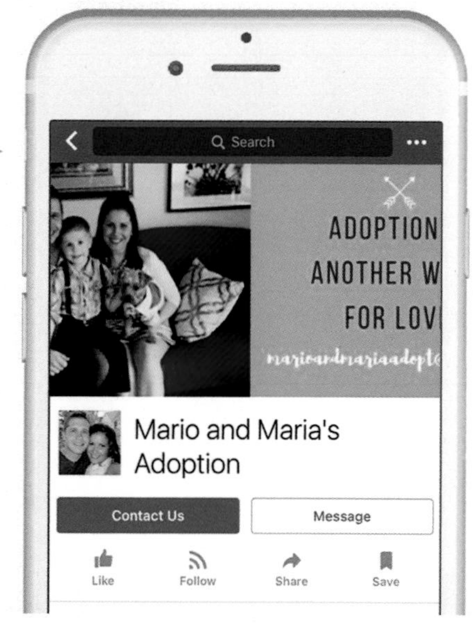

3. COVER PHOTO GENERATOR There are many different places online that will help you create a Facebook cover photo, and most of the time at no or little cost!

A FEW PLACES TO LOOK:

- PicMonkey.com
- Canva.com
- Pagemodo.com

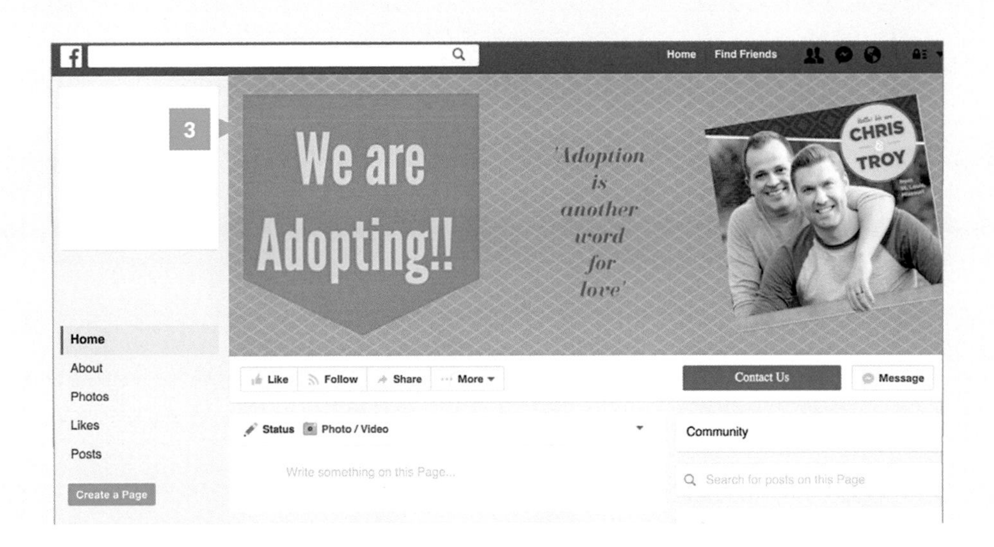

▲ *Facebook cover photo*

THE IMPORTANCE OF BRANDING *While using a free Facebook template can be fun, keep in mind that you can also use this as a place to reinforce your personal branding. Meaning, your cover photo can have the same look as your adoption profile, your outreach cards, your blog/website/Hopefully Parents page, etc. This way, anyone who visits will get to see the same familiar family and that consistency builds trust and comfort. Several of the outreach packages available on HopefullyParents.com include the creation of a custom (or matching) Facebook cover photo!*

▲ *Adoption profile (cover)*

▲ *Pull-tab flyer*

▲ *Outreach cards (double-sided)*

HOPEFULLY PARENTS

HOPEFULLYPARENTS.COM

FACEBOOK

Sharing your adoption outreach page.

EVERYTHING IS SET UP, *and your page is officially complete. Congratulations, now comes the fun part! You can share your page with Facebook friends, start posting content and discover ways to increase your audience! The larger your audience, the larger your reach will be when sharing content, so focus on gaining "likes" right away!*

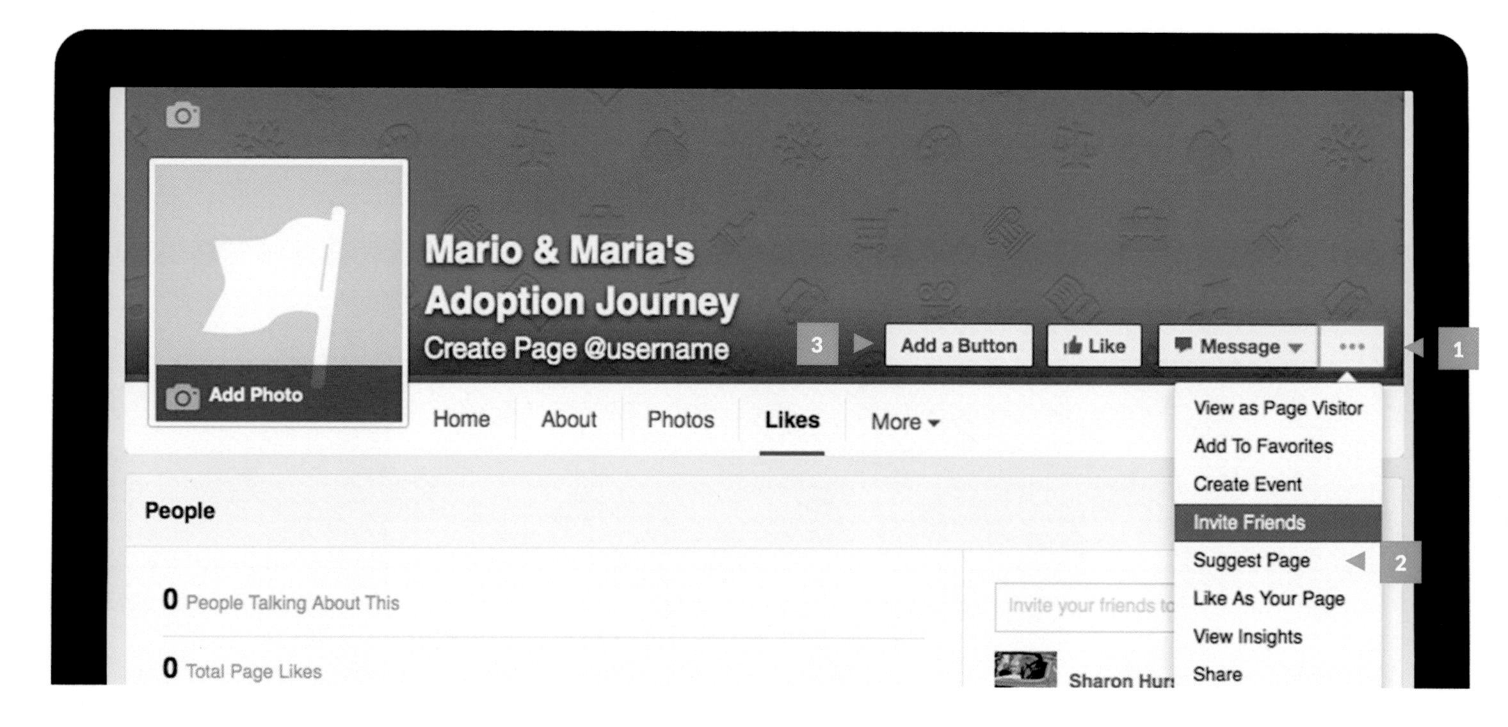

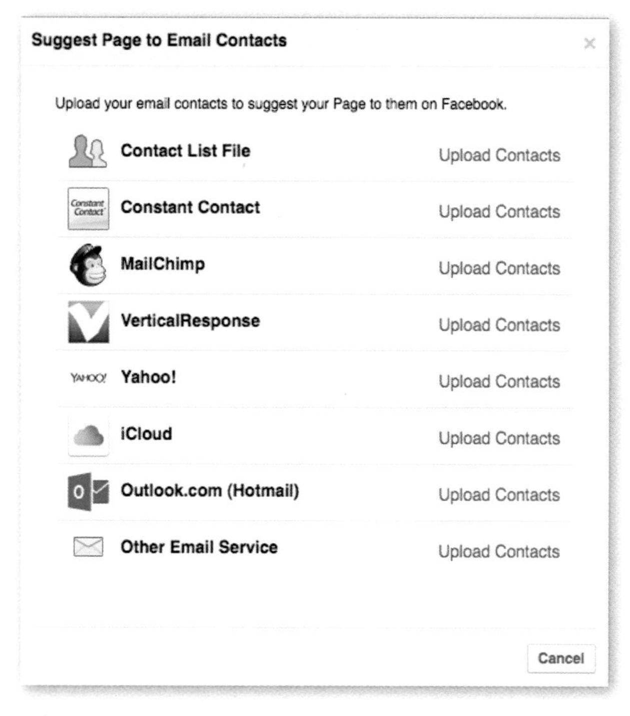

Suggest page to email contacts

TWO WAYS TO GROW YOUR PAGE'S REACH

1. INVITE FACEBOOK FRIENDS Now that your page is set up, it's time to invite your friends to your page so they can read your information and stay up-to-date on your journey. If you have a personal Facebook page you will be able to invite your friends to "like" your new adoption-specific community page.

   NOTE: With a personal page people must make a "friend request" to follow your page, but with a community page people can just "like" your page to follow you.

2. SUGGEST PAGE TO EMAIL CONTACTS You can use your email contacts and invite any of your contacts to your page as well. When you click "Suggest Page" this box will appear (see left) and walk you through the process of uploading email contacts in order to invite them to your page.

3. ADD A 'CONTACT US' BUTTON Make sure to set up a way for people to contact you in case an expectant parent wants to get in touch. You can include multiple contact methods such as phone, email, text, etc.

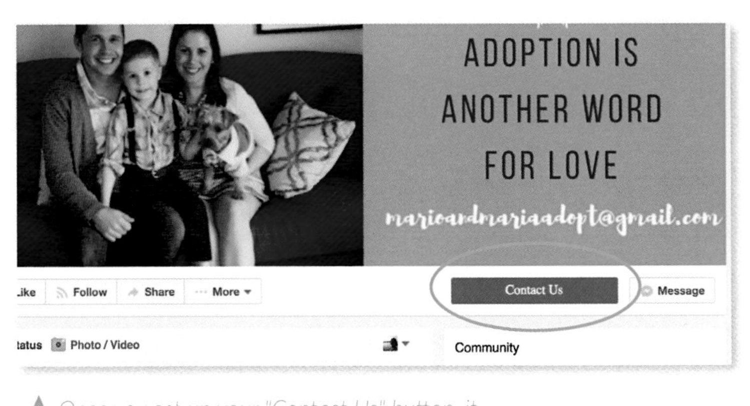

Once you set up your "Contact Us" button, it will appear right below your cover photo

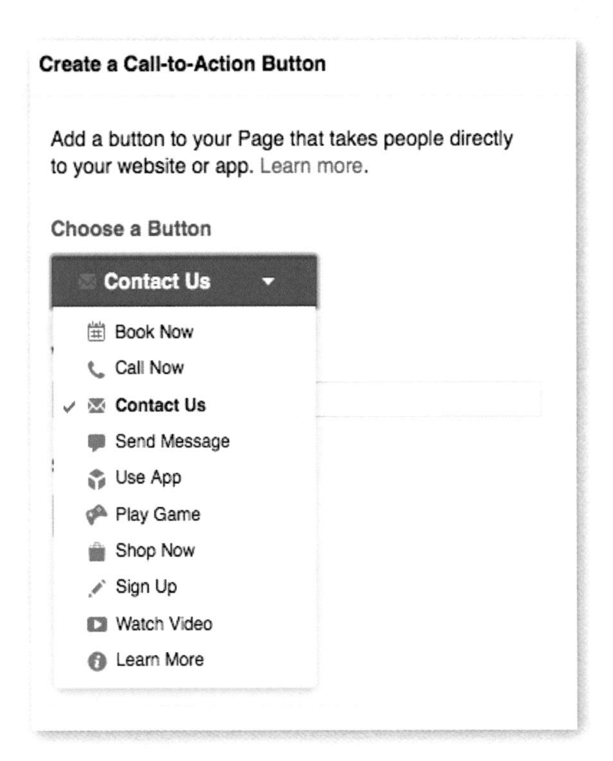

Once you set up your "Contact Us" button

BECOME AN ACTIVE USER

Once your page is all set up and you have invited friends and family members to "share" and "like" your page, you will want to continue your progress.

You will want to engage in the larger Facebook community to expand your network and make more connections. A great place to start is by engaging in the active adoption community on Facebook. You can do this at the individual level by searching for other hopeful adoptive parents and "liking" their pages. Be sure to be friendly and comment on their posts and they will likely do the same for you! Liking other adoption pages is also a great way to see what other hopeful adoptive parents are posting and sharing!

At a more global level you can join Facebook groups related to adoption. Some groups are just for hopeful adoptive parents and others are geared to more specific aspects of adoption like trans-racial adoption. There's a great, already established community on Facebook, so dig in and start engaging!

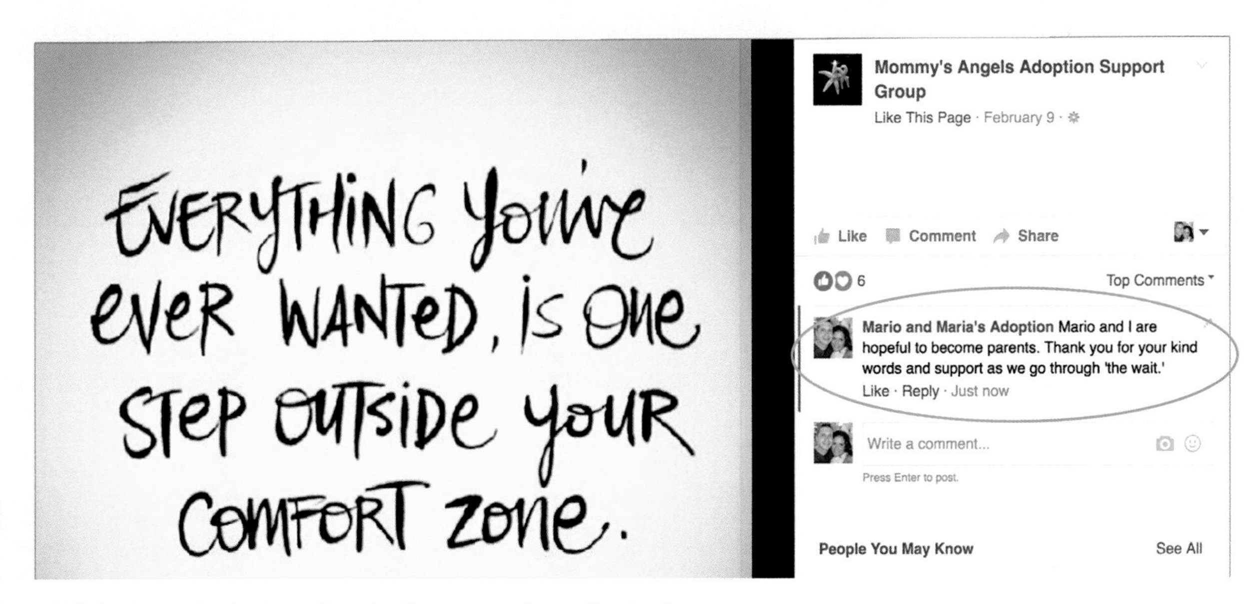

Maria and Michael engaging in the active adoption community on Facebook

FACEBOOK

Feeling stuck when thinking about what to post on your page?

FOR MAXIMUM VISIBILITY ***your goal is to get your Facebook community page to show up in your friends' news feed. This will only happen when they "interact" with your page. Because of this, we recommend posting content 3-5 times per week to engage with your followers. Here are some suggestions for posts that will encourage or initiate conversations and activity on your page.***

- Make a movie! Video is the latest outreach tool for adoption. Learn how to make a video through easy-to-use sites like Animoto and post them to your page, as well as other social media sites. For video tips and help to get started, see page 46 in this book.

  SUGGESTION: *If you have an older child at home (or favorite niece/nephew), have them shoot a video for you! Harness the power of a pre-teen and their knowledge of video editing and social media. It could be a fun "why my parents want to be parents again" video or a "sneak peek at my folks best (or worst!) kitchen dance routine." You may not go viral, but you will have fun!*

- Common things unite us all, such as food. If you are trying a new recipe, or looking for one, this is a great time to engage with your followers. Consider a repeating post like, "What's for dinner Wednesday" where you share your menu and ask others to share theirs!

- It's okay to ask for help on how to do something or fix things because people love to offer their help. You could ask how to change a setting on your phone or what to do if you can't resist buying girl scout cookies for the 10th time. Some can be serious and some can be a little more lighthearted and fun.

- You could post a 'joke of the week.' Mind the content and appropriateness, but a lot of people love corny, one-line jokes that elicit a groan.

- If you have any traveling adventures, make sure to share where you went or what you enjoyed. Some folks don't like to share these things while they are actually away (for security reasons), but you can share once you get back home. It doesn't have to be a big getaway; just a new destination can create interesting comments. Did you find a great donut shop? Did you discover a new bike trail to ride? Did you just visit friends and have a good time catching up? Share these kinds of things!

  NOTE: *Be sure to TAG people in your photos and CHECK IN places when you do things (like at a concert, movie, etc.), so your posts show up in other people's news feed. This increases your exposure exponentially because your page name (e.g., Bill and Ted are Adopting!) will show up along with your interesting comment.*

- Post a "question meme" to elicit responses. We've provided the graphics below on both our Hopefully Parents Facebook page and on our Bright Ideas blog www.hopefullyparents.com/brightideas

Thanks to Kelly Shade and her Facebook group "Private or Independent Adoption Support Group" ▶

- Share a dream or something you can't wait to do once you are a parent to engage your audience. It could be something like: "I heard the ice cream truck come down the street tonight. I can't wait to run out there with my child and pick a special treat together. My favorite is bomb pops! What's your favorite?"

- A lot of people use their Facebook page as a way to keep friends and family members updated on their adoption progress, so don't forget to give an update every now and then on what is happening. Have any contact with a birth family? Still working on a nursery? Completing a home study? Let them know!

- Use your community page audience as a great source for advice and ideas. Trying to figure out what to buy your teenage nephew for Christmas? Want to know the best snacks to serve for your upcoming party? Looking for a new website to buy shoes? Reach out and ask!

- Have you ever noticed how much people love animals? That's right, use the power of puppies, kittens or funny animal stories to warm hearts and share stories!

- Do you enjoy watching sports or have a favorite team? Feel free to brag about their game or cheer them on!

- Did you stumble upon an organizational tip or a way to creatively use a household item? Share your new discovery and see what others can contribute as well.

√ Maria likes to share funny little stories to engage her audience such as, "I saw a mouse run behind my kitchen sink cabinet and jumped up on the counter to get away from it. I threw a cookbook down just trying to scare it away and bingo, squashed mouse. So much for good aim! What would you have done in this situation?"

- Share some memories or traditions with a photo! Here's a chance to share a bit more about yourself and engage your audience. Share a photo of your uncle fishing at the cabin and talk about your yearly family vacation at the lake with s'mores and campfires. Share a photo of your mom cutting your hair as a kid and how every Sunday was bath and haircut night growing up. Think of fun little stories to share and get people to laugh with you, reminisce with you or share their own stories as well.

- Play a game! There are lots of fun things like guessing games that can be played. Take a close up photo of something in the nursery and ask "What is this?" and see if people can guess. Give it a few hours and then share the answer. Or think about asking trivia questions (like Jeopardy!), pricing questions (The Price Is Right) or top answers to popular topics (Family Feud). There are so many ways to get creative playing a game and making it a regular "feature" on your page!

HELPFUL HINT

YOU CAN SCHEDULE POSTS TO APPEAR ON YOUR PAGE RATHER THAN SIGNING IN EVERY DAY. CLICK THE ARROW NEXT TO 'PUBLISH' AND SELECT SCHEDULE.

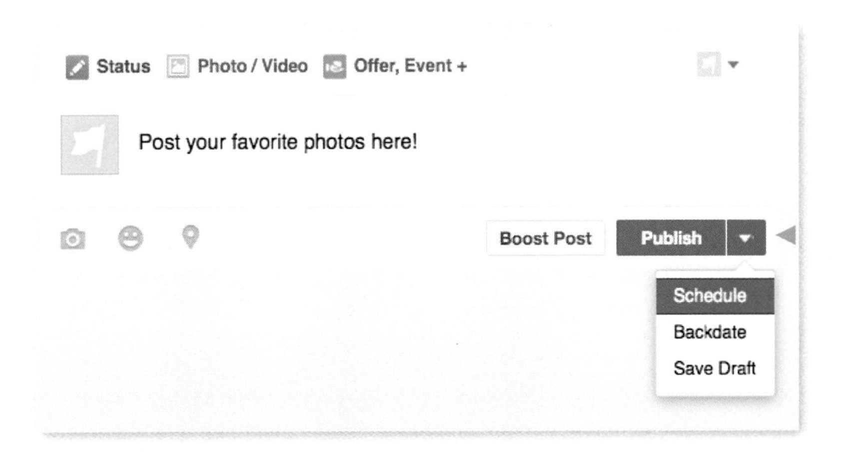

FACEBOOK

An interview with clients Hillary and Joel.

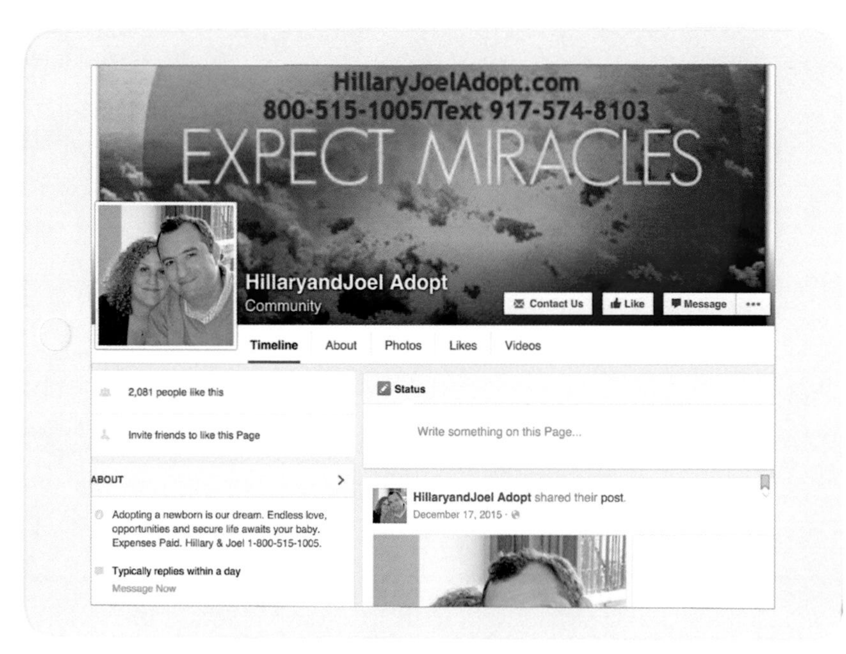

▲ *A glimpse of the facebook page that Hillary and Joel used*

HILLARY AND JOEL ***are a couple from New York who decided to pursue a private adoption with the help of an adoption attorney, Laurie Goldheim. Their outreach plan included an adoption profile and custom website developed by Our Chosen Child, as well as a Facebook community page that they managed on their own.***

HOW DID YOUR ADOPTION OUTREACH DIFFER FROM YOUR EXPECTATIONS?

In the beginning I thought I didn't know enough about the adoption process to do it successfully. I didn't know the first thing about using Facebook or having a website, and I never dreamed I would be using both on a daily basis, but I did! I'm even on Instagram now.

CAN YOU TELL US ABOUT HOW YOU BEGAN DOING ADOPTION OUTREACH?

When we started I wasn't sure what I was doing, so I just kept notes on what was working best and spent more time doing those things. I was scared that being on Facebook would lead to scams, so we signed up with a popular website for adoptive families instead.

Laurie Goldheim's law office is dedicated exclusively to the practice of adoption law. Laurie has been helping many couples and individuals build their families and realize their dreams through adoption for over 15 years.

For more information, visit: www.adoptionrights.com

We even did a billboard on the New Jersey turnpike! We weren't getting the results that we wanted so we started using Facebook. Once we did that we realized that we were getting a lot more attention and contact than we were from the other sources, so we focused our energy there. We did get a few scams, but no more than our other outreach methods.

HOW DID YOU USE FACEBOOK FOR YOUR OUTREACH?

I really learned as I went. I spent more than an hour a day on Facebook. I would post cute little inspirational messages or I would make a collage with our photo, "hoping to adopt" and our website and text number. If someone would "like" or comment on a post, I would comment on their page saying "Thank you for liking our page! It means a lot to us because we are hoping to adopt." This would often start a dialogue with the person with nice messages like "We're praying for you." I would make a note on my calendar and then circle back to them in a couple weeks to follow up.

HOW DID YOU USE FACEBOOK FOR YOUR OUTREACH? (CONTINUED)

I also went onto all sorts of Facebook pages and would post our photo and message. I would go onto pro-life Facebook groups and pro-life college groups. Sometimes they would ignore me and sometimes they would offer to help which was great. I found Pennsylvania and Texas have lots of pro-life groups by the way!

I also did a lot of boosting posts and promoting our page. When I selected audiences for the promoted posts, I would choose people who liked popular shows like "Teen Mom," "16 and Pregnant," "She's Carrying our Baby," and search terms like "OMG I'm pregnant!" or "abortion or adoption." I would spend around $700 a month on promoting our page and posts. I just kept track of which posts got the most likes and then I would do more of whatever had been successful. I was relentless, I guess you could say. One of my boosted posts got 2,100 "likes" so I would say it worked!

I used to post things like "What does adoption mean to you?" and I would get lots and lots of responses. I would try to think of questions people would want to answer, and then I would always reply to their comment and try to start a conversation.

WHAT WAS THE FEEDBACK YOU RECEIVED AND DID YOU HAVE ANY CONTACT WITH EXPECTANT PARENTS?

We were constantly communicating with people. This really surprised me, especially in the beginning. We had so many people contact us to say "My friend/cousin/sister is pregnant and in a terrible situation. I'm going to give her your website." We thought that was great, but we just said "thank you" and gave them some space. I did follow up with them awhile later but none of those panned out. We got a lot of contact from people that weren't pregnant, but knew of someone who was. Knowing that helped me broaden my search terms when I was advertising on Facebook so I could look beyond just pregnant people looking at adoption.

Overall I think a lot of people with a crisis pregnancy will go onto Facebook and click around, but they aren't necessarily looking for adoptive parents. I tried to post in places where they would see us as they were surfing on Facebook, and that seemed to work out well. I think they would use Facebook as a way to be in contact with friends and search for things that interested them, so I tried to think like an expectant parent and tried to be on the same pages she might be.

I also discovered that there are a lot of people that are willing to help you if you just ask. At first it was friends and family but as we got more "likes" it was total strangers that would share our page, and that made me feel really good.

HOW DID YOU ULTIMATELY CONNECT WITH YOUR SON'S BIRTH FAMILY?

Our attorney suggested placing ads in places like "The Penny Saver," so we did some of that too. Out of the blue we got a call from a mom whose daughter was pregnant, and that connection ultimately led to our son. I really think if we hadn't met our son's birth family that my work on Facebook would have led to a match too. We got really close a couple of times and had a lot of great feedback. In fact we had so many "likes" on our Facebook page we started using it to help promote other adoptive families.

▲ *Hillary and Joel's son, Levi*

FACEBOOK

Paid advertising options on Facebook.

ADVERTISING *is another way to increase your audience on Facebook. Getting your page noticed by posting, commenting and sharing is fantastic, but by using paid advertising, you can reach a much wider group of people. You will be fishing in a larger lake, so to speak. There are many different advertising options available on Facebook. Let's take an in-depth look at the three most helpful options below.*

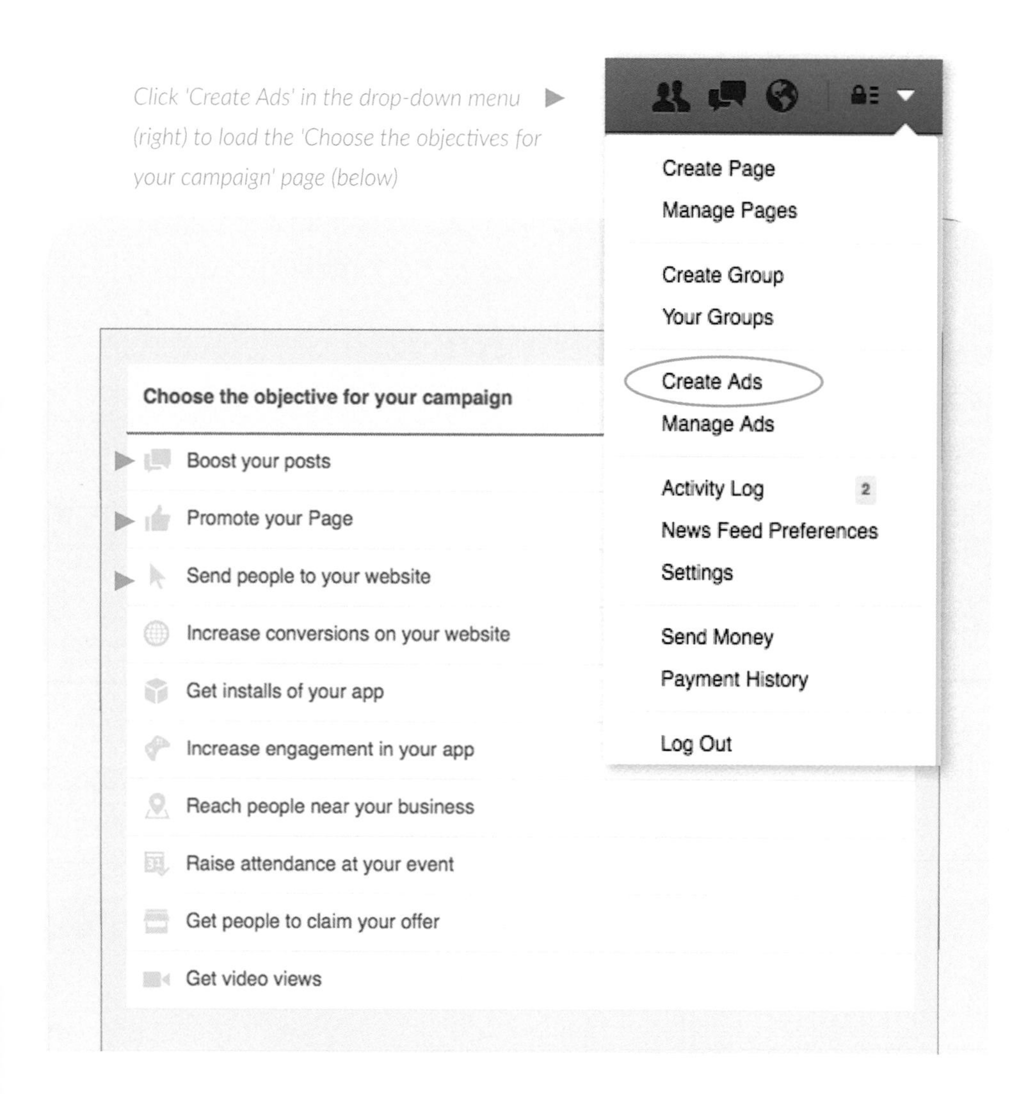

Click 'Create Ads' in the drop-down menu (right) to load the 'Choose the objectives for your campaign' page (below)

- BOOST YOUR POSTS This option allows you to boost the visibility of a specific post you create on your page. The goal is to introduce your community page to the friends of people who already "liked" it and read your page.
- PROMOTE YOUR PAGE This option will get people over to your page and "liking" it so they become aware that it exists. It's still up to you to keep them engaged and to post on the page regularly so it continues to appear in their news feeds. This is your best option!
- SEND PEOPLE TO YOUR WEBSITE This option encourages people to click over to your website (or blog) to learn more about you. If you don't capture their interest on your website (or blog), you have no way to connect to them again.

DISCLAIMER:

HOPEFULLY PARENTS IS NEITHER RESPONSIBLE FOR, NOR AUTHORIZED TO GIVE LEGAL ADVICE RELATING TO ADOPTION ADVERTISING.

HOPEFULLY PARENTS ENCOURAGES YOU TO CHECK WITH YOUR STATE ATTORNEY OR AGENCY BEFORE ADVERTISING IN YOUR STATE (OR BEYOND.)

FACEBOOK

How to set up an ad in order to promote your community page.

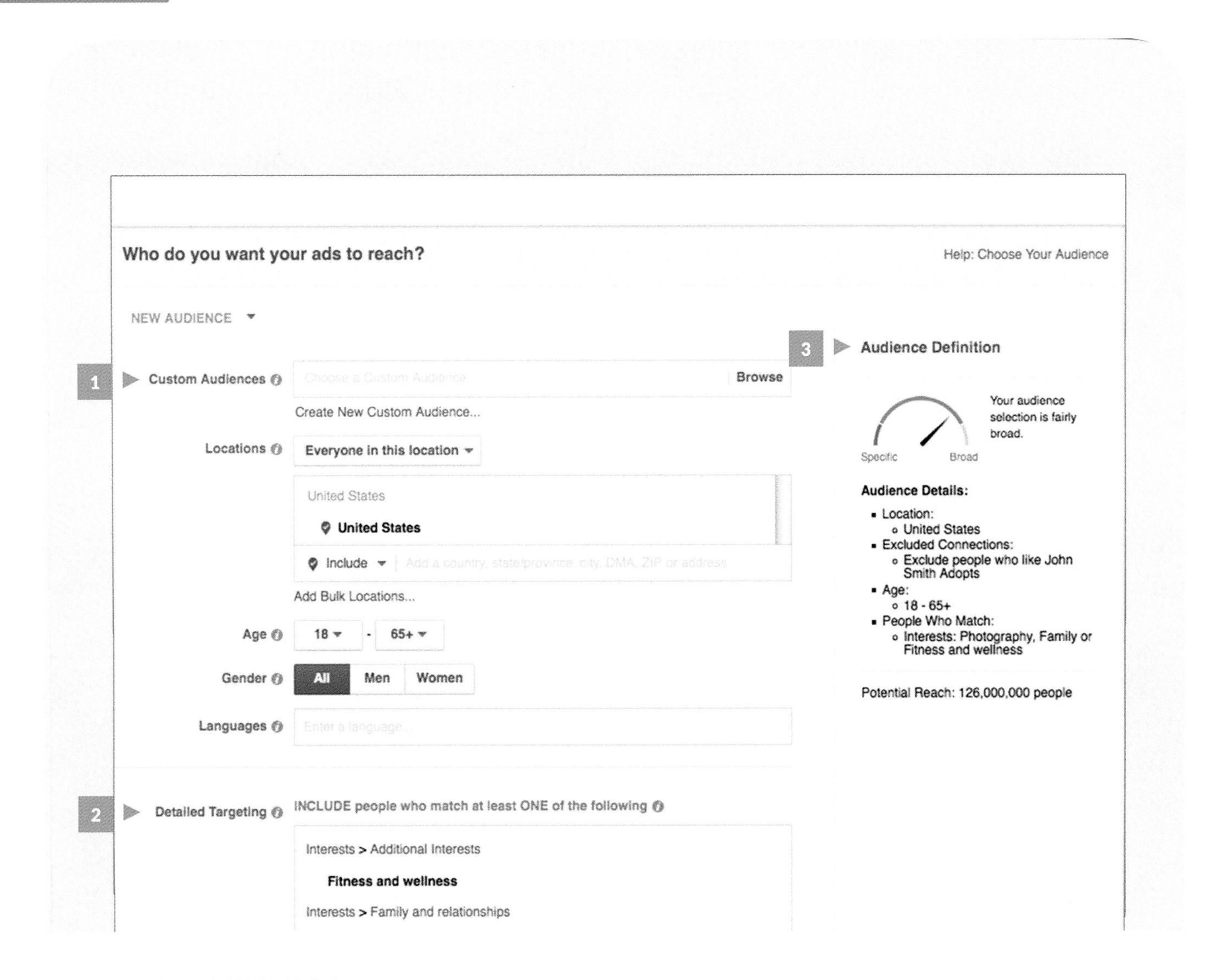

OPTIONS & SETTINGS

1. CUSTOM AUDIENCE: You can set the age range and gender for the audience of your ad. Do not just appeal to young, expectant parents! It might be that a mom or aunt knows of someone with a crisis pregnancy that might consider adoption. You can also set the geographic location where your ad is shown and not shown. We recommend you OMIT states where advertising is not allowed (please refer to page 29) unless specifically directed by your attorney. Be sure to check with your attorney first.

RUN SEVERAL ADS WITH DIFFERENT CUSTOM AUDIENCES AND SEE WHICH ONES GET THE MOST TRACTION!

2. DETAILED TARGETING: You can use your keywords to connect to people that share your interests or lifestyle choices. You can get really specific and choose multiple topics for your audience. The more specific you can be, the more likely you will be to make a meaningful connection!

3. AUDIENCE DEFINITION: This tool helps you to gauge how broad or specific your settings are. Facebook thinks, as do we, that being specific is better than being too vague. It's a great way to monitor your selections!

FACEBOOK

Set up your Facebook ad to send people to your website or Hopefully Parents page.

IF YOU HAVE A WEBSITE *or blog that you want people to visit, you can run an ad to encourage visitors. We have found this option to be helpful only if you are active on your blog or have different content on your website than you do on your Facebook page so there is new, relevant and engaging content for your visitors. If you have a Hopefully Parents page, this option will showcase your profile, video and photo gallery!*

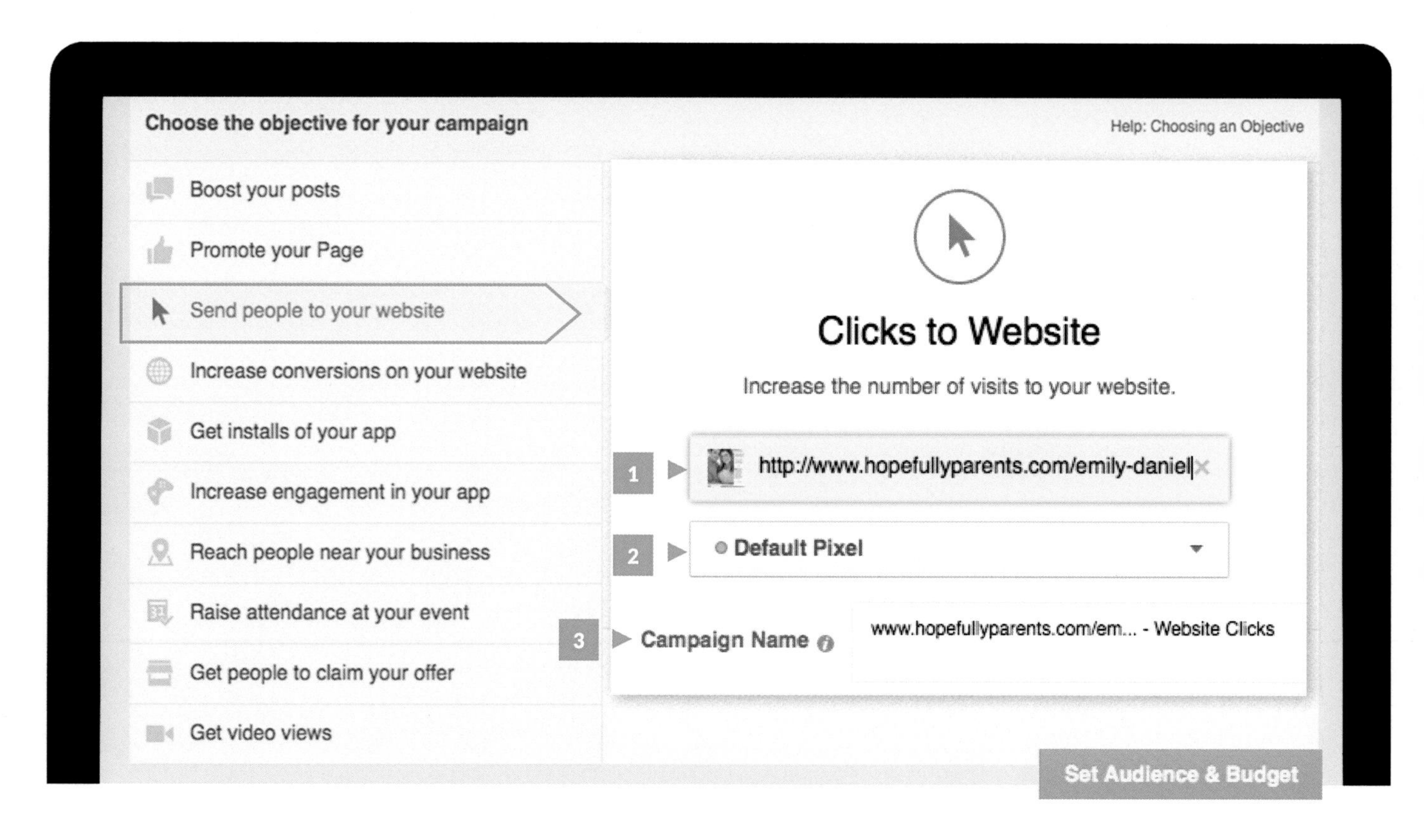

SEND PEOPLE TO YOUR WEBSITE

1. LIST THE WEB ADDRESS (URL) to the website where you want people to be directed. This can be your Hopefully Parents page, a website that you created or a blog. Make sure to list the web address correctly.

2. DEFAULT PIXEL: This option creates a code for tracking and analyzing traffic from Facebook to your website or link. Facebook will walk you through how to create this pixel. You only need one pixel per ad campaign. There is a help button right on this page for more information on how to set up a pixel. Adding a pixel is optional, but helpful!

3. CAMPAIGN NAME: It is helpful to name your campaign so you can track results and fine-tune further ads you might run. You might name your campaign with details about the ad you are running or the audience you selected. You can have more than one campaign running at a time and more than one ad associated with a campaign. For example, you might have one ad to get new people to click over to your website and that campaign would be "More Website Traffic." You could also have another ad running at the same time under the campaign "More FB Page Likes" which is promoting your Facebook page.

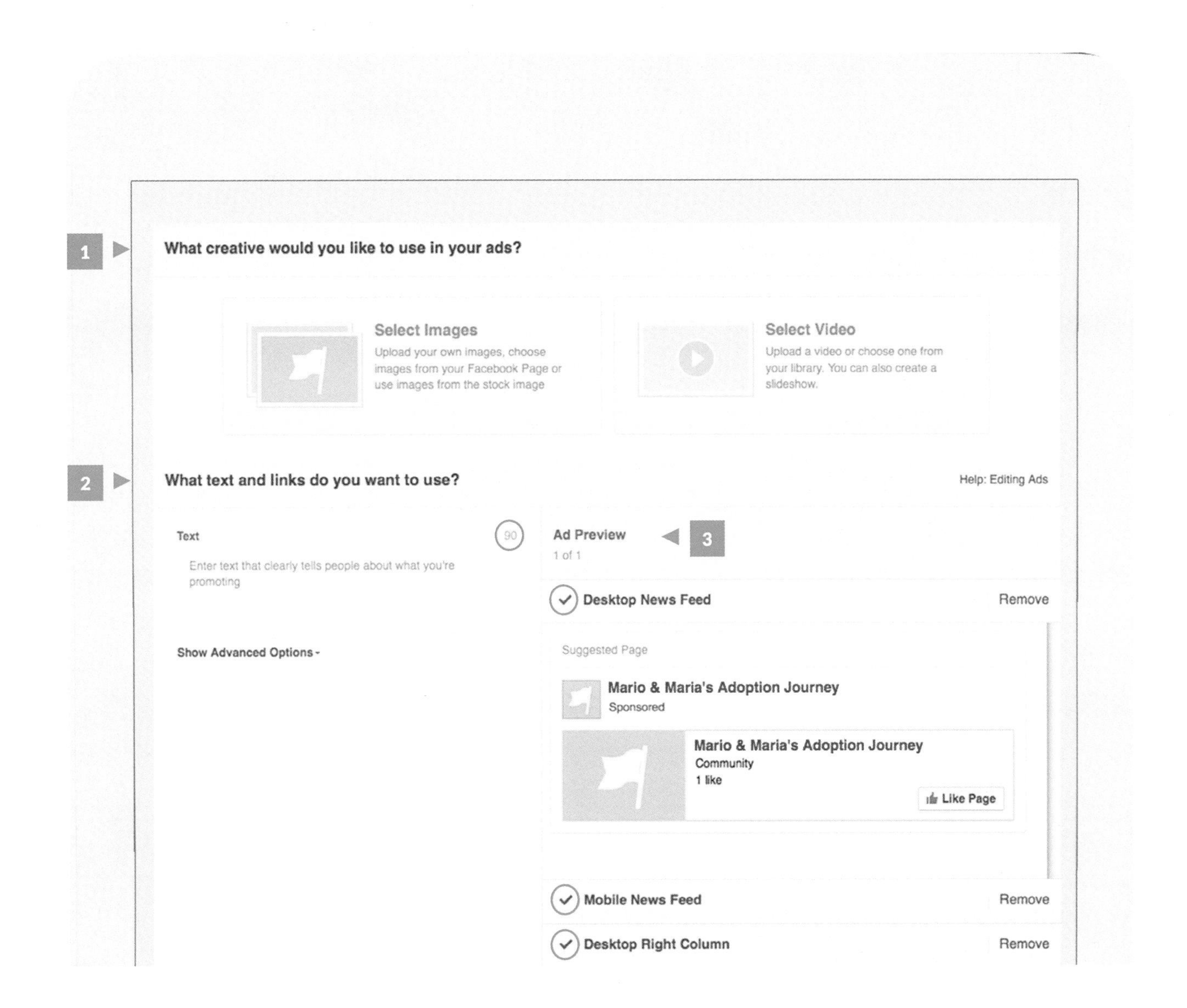

OPTIONS & SETTINGS

1. CREATIVE OPTIONS FOR ADS: Select a picture or video that you would like to incorporate into your ad. This could be an image from your website/blog, an image with text overlay you create yourself or a photo of you. Bright and fun photos where you take up 75% of the frame are best. Avoid sunglasses or hats, people want to see your eyes and your smile!

2. TEXT AND LINKS: Write a short description or add your perfected ad copy right here to appear by your image/video in your ad. This is like a text message; you only have 90 characters available to use. There is a handy counter keeping track for you and it will let you know if you run out of space.

3. AD PREVIEW: This gives you the chance to view your ad as it will appear on different devices, such as a phone or computer. You have the opportunity to fix anything that might not be displaying in a manner that you like. You can choose Desktop News Feed, Mobile News Feed and Desktop Right Column to preview your ad.

NOTE: *If you use an image with text overlay the text must not cover more than 20% of the image. Facebook will not show your ad if there is too much text! The ad above is an image within the 20% rule.*

FACEBOOK

How to set up your ad in order to boost your post in the news feed.

DID YOU KNOW *that not all posts from a community page get shown to all people? Paying to boost a post ensures your post will appear in others' news feeds. There are two ways to boost a post in Facebook. One is to go through the Ads Manager and the other option is to write a post directly on your community page and boost it from there. With either option you will get to set up a budget, specific audience, length to run, etc. Let's look at both ways to books a post!*

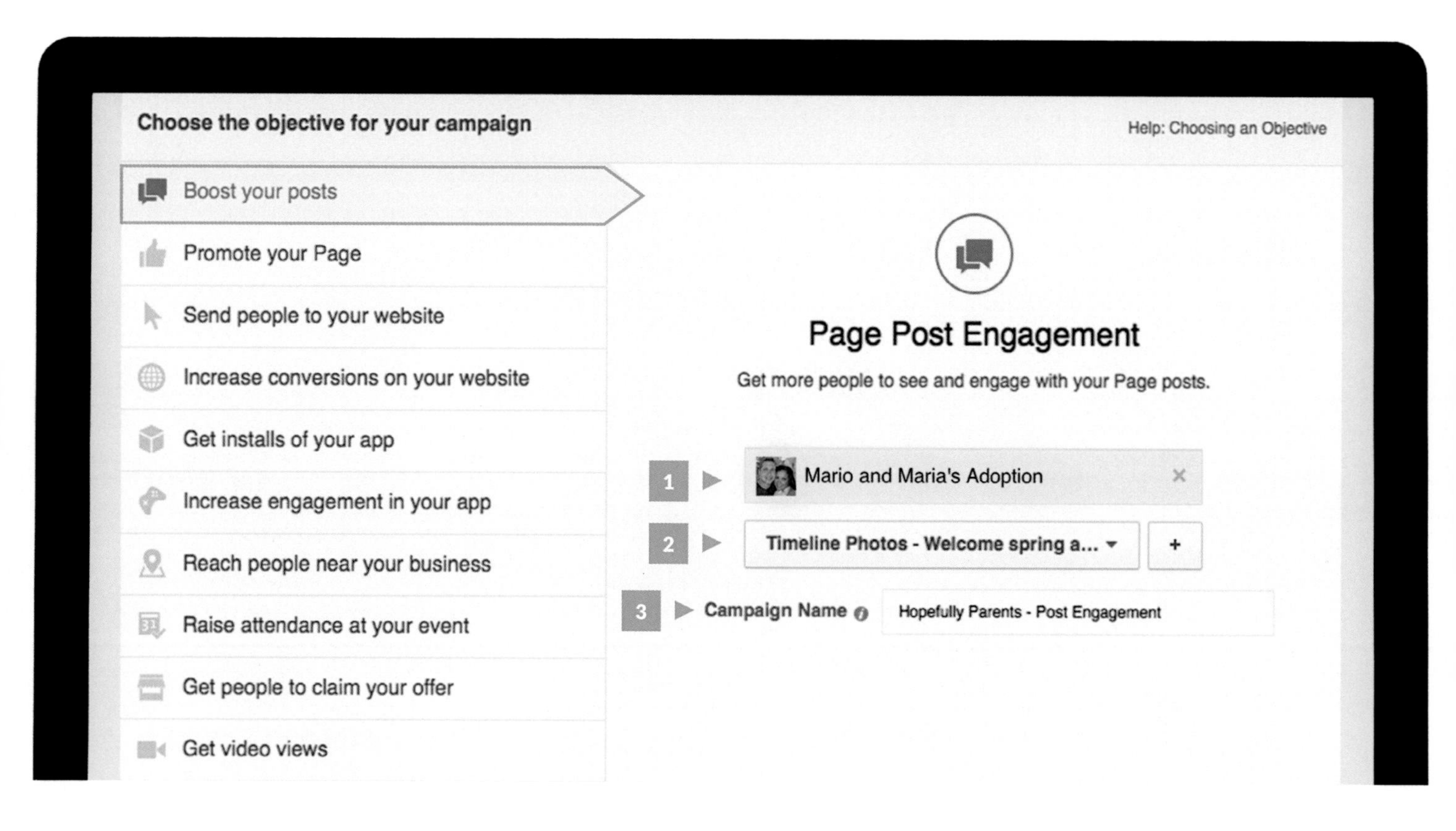

BOOSTING A POST FROM AD MANAGER

1. SELECT THE ACCOUNT If you have both a personal and adoption-specific Facebook page, you will be able to toggle here to select your adoption-specific page.

2. SELECT YOUR POST By clicking on the drop-down box, you will see a list of your most recent posts on the page that you selected. If there is one here that you want to boost, choose it. If you want to write a new post to boost, click on the "+" button to write something new.

3. CAMPAIGN NAME You need to give your campaign a name and, since you may be running several ads at once, it's helpful to be specific in the name you create for the campaign. For example, you might name a campaign with the goal of the post ("encourage comments") or with the content of the post ("Introducing Mario.")

BOOST POSTS WHEN YOU KNOW YOU WILL BE NEAR YOUR PHONE OR COMPUTER SO YOU CAN REPLY PROMPTLY TO ANY COMMENTS OR QUESTIONS FROM YOUR AUDIENCE!

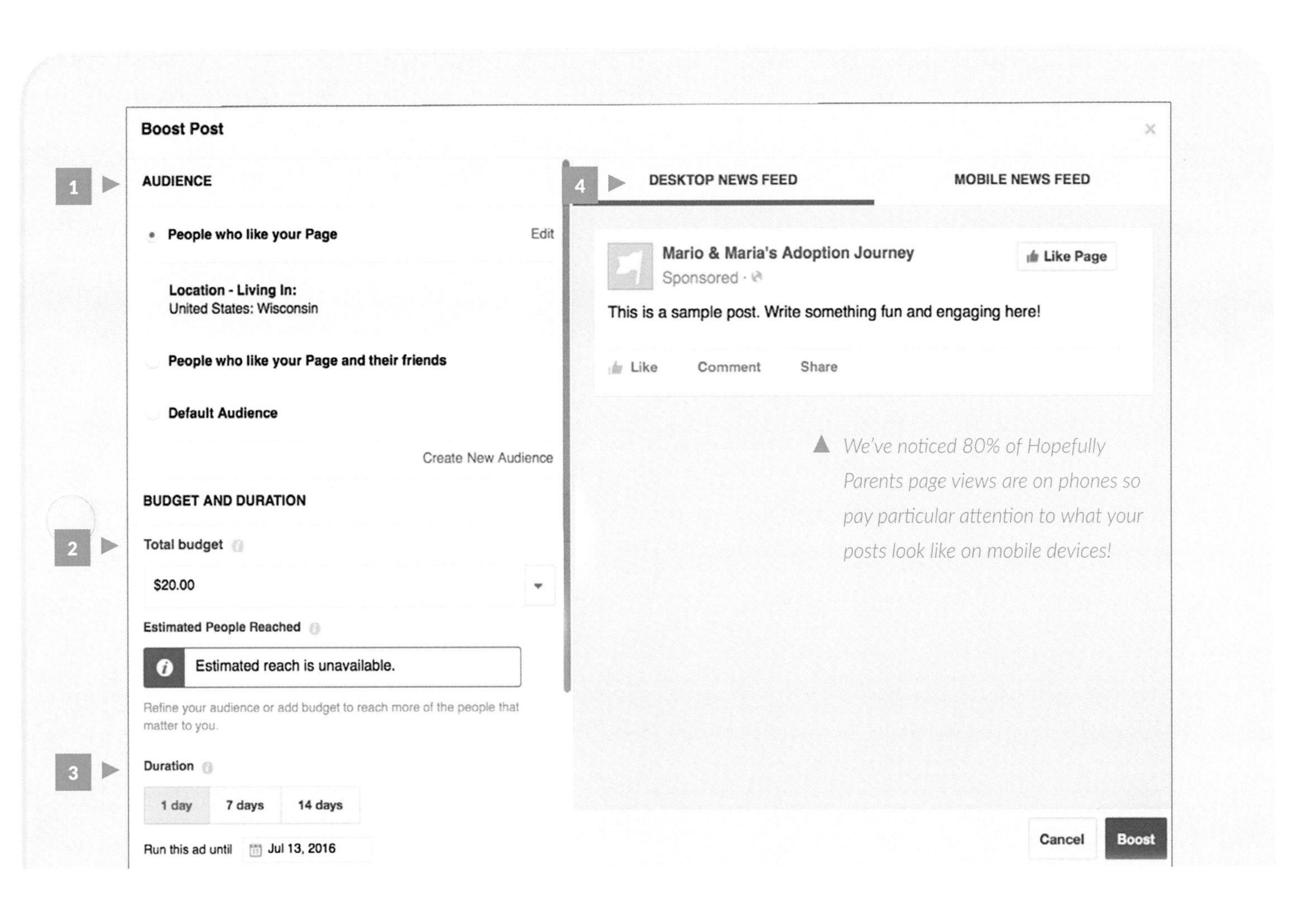

▲ *We've noticed 80% of Hopefully Parents page views are on phones so pay particular attention to what your posts look like on mobile devices!*

OPTIONS & SETTINGS

1. AUDIENCE: You can create a specific audience for each post or use one you've already set up and saved.

2. BUDGET: Play with your budget and see what gives you the most impact; boosting several posts for a small amount or spending a larger budget on just one post. Keep notes and spend more on future posts similar to the ones getting the most traction.

3. DURATION: The duration is how long you want the post to be boosted. Start with shorter durations so you can gauge the impact of your posts. Once you know what works you can run longer promotions for higher budget amounts.

4. DESKTOP OR MOBILE NEWSFEED: This will give you a preview of what your post will look like when viewed on a computer or mobile device. Click on the "DESKTOP NEWS FEED" to see a preview when viewed from a computer and click on "MOBILE NEWS FEED" to see a preview when viewed on a mobile phone.

BOOST DIRECTLY FROM YOUR PAGE

Anytime you post you have the option of boosting that post right away via the "boost post" button. You have the same options for selecting an audience and budget for your post. It's helpful to have pre-set audiences ready so you can boost posts on the fly!

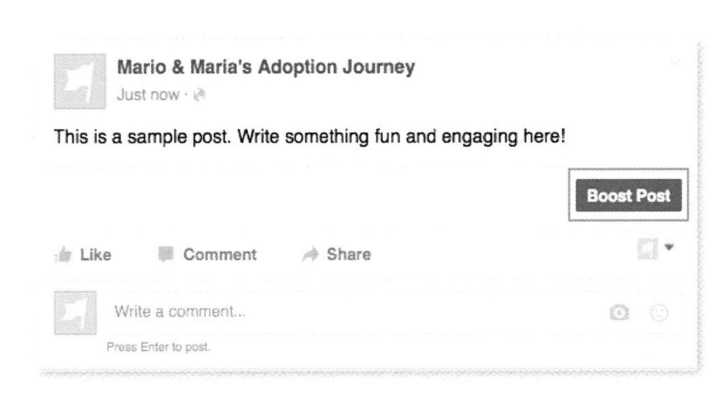

▲ *You can boost any post directly from your community page by clicking on the "Boost Post" button.*

FACEBOOK

How to use Facebook Stories

CONNECT ON A CLOSER LEVEL ***Facebook Stories are short user-generated photo and video collections that can be viewed up to two times and disappear after 24 hours. You can share stories with your friends within the main Facebook app, similar to SnapChat. Facebook Stories allow you to overlay fun filters and Snapchat-like lenses to your content as well as add visual geolocation tags to your photos and videos!***

1. HOW FACEBOOK STORIES WORK Content shared to stories will appear at the top of the Facebook News Feed. To view a story, users simply tap a friends' circle at the top of the app. While viewing a story, users can also reply with a direct message.

HOW TO ADD CONTENT TO FACEBOOK STORIES:

2. ACCESS THE CAMERA To create a story on Facebook, you first need to access the camera. You can do this by swiping right on the Facebook mobile app.

3. CREATE YOUR CONTENT You can share both photos and videos to stories. Once you have the camera open, you'll be able to record your video or snap a quick photo. You'll also notice a range of lenses and filters available to embellish your content.

To take a photo, tap on the button in the center of the screen and to record a video hold down this button.

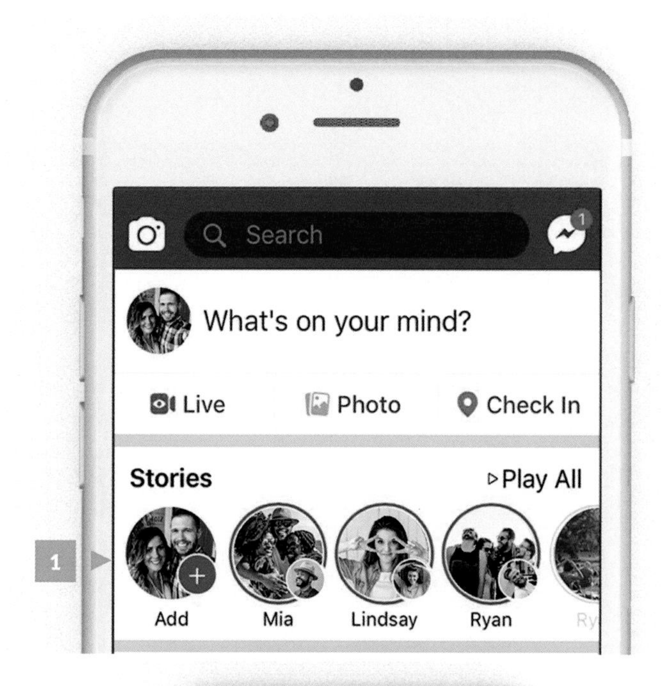

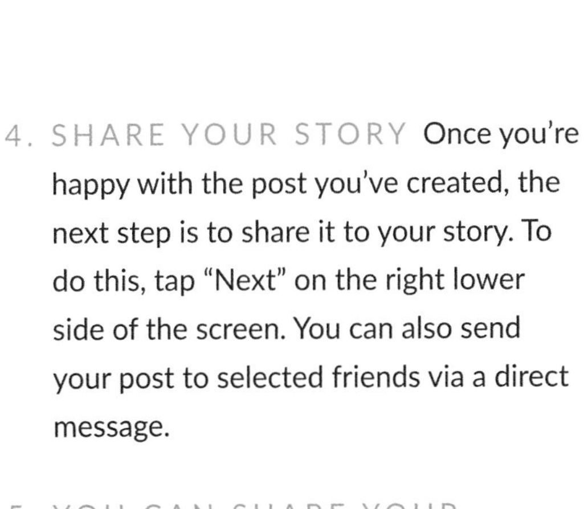

4. SHARE YOUR STORY Once you're happy with the post you've created, the next step is to share it to your story. To do this, tap "Next" on the right lower side of the screen. You can also send your post to selected friends via a direct message.

5. YOU CAN SHARE YOUR STORY TO YOUR TIMELINE By selecting "Post" under "Your Story" you can make your story appear directly on your timeline. This will not automatically delete after 24 hours.

6. YOU CAN ALSO SEND YOUR POST TO SELECTED FRIENDS VIA A DIRECT MESSAGE Scroll down and select what friend(s) you'd like to send your Story directly to.

7. TO SEND YOUR STORY Press the blue button in the lower right corner Once you've shared a post to your story, it will display for 24 hours and then be gone forever. Videos and photos posted in a Facebook Story won't show up in the News Feed or on a user's timeline by default, but users can choose to share to the News Feed as well if they'd like to (See step 5).

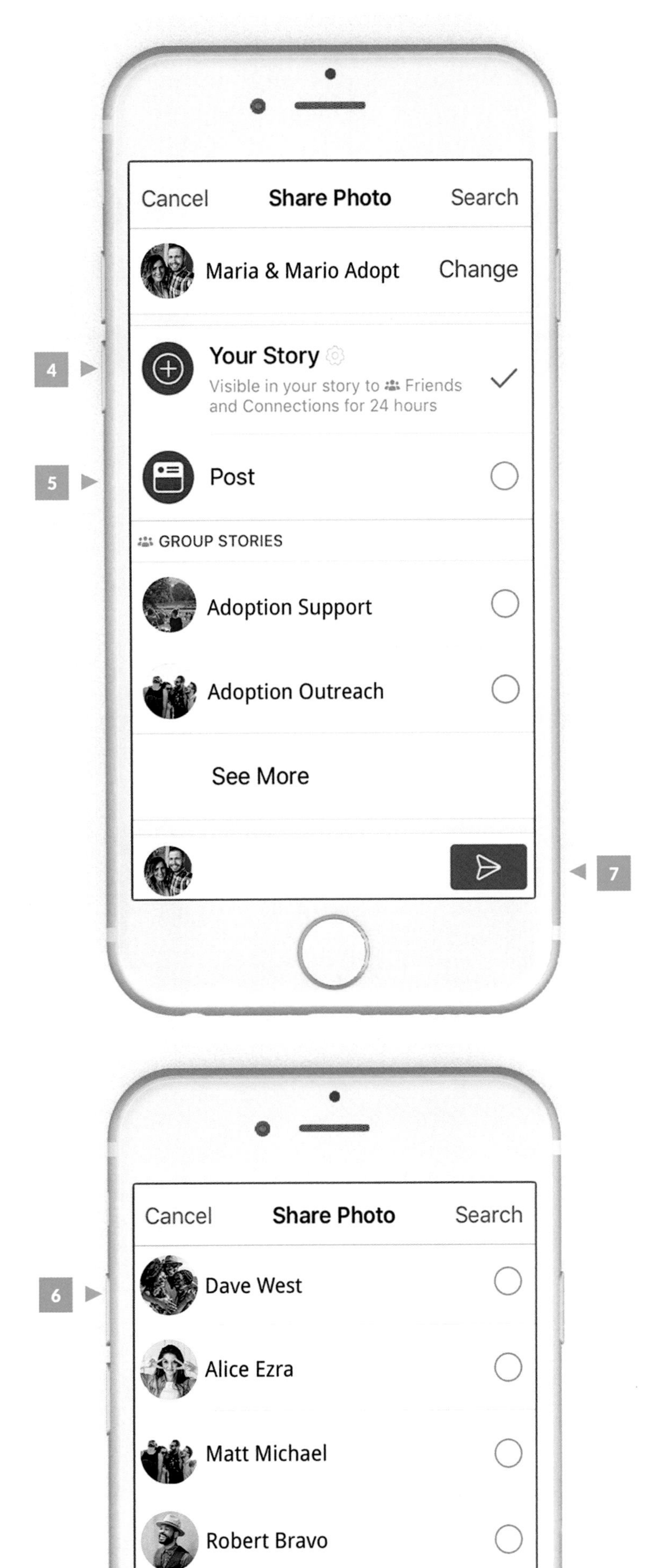

TWITTER

How to set up an account.

WHAT'S A TWEET? ***If you haven't experienced the world of Twitter, you're in for a treat. Twitter is a free and easy way to build a network of people with common interests and to share succinct, interesting "tweets" with a larger audience. Let's take a look at how to set up a Twitter account and begin your adventure!***

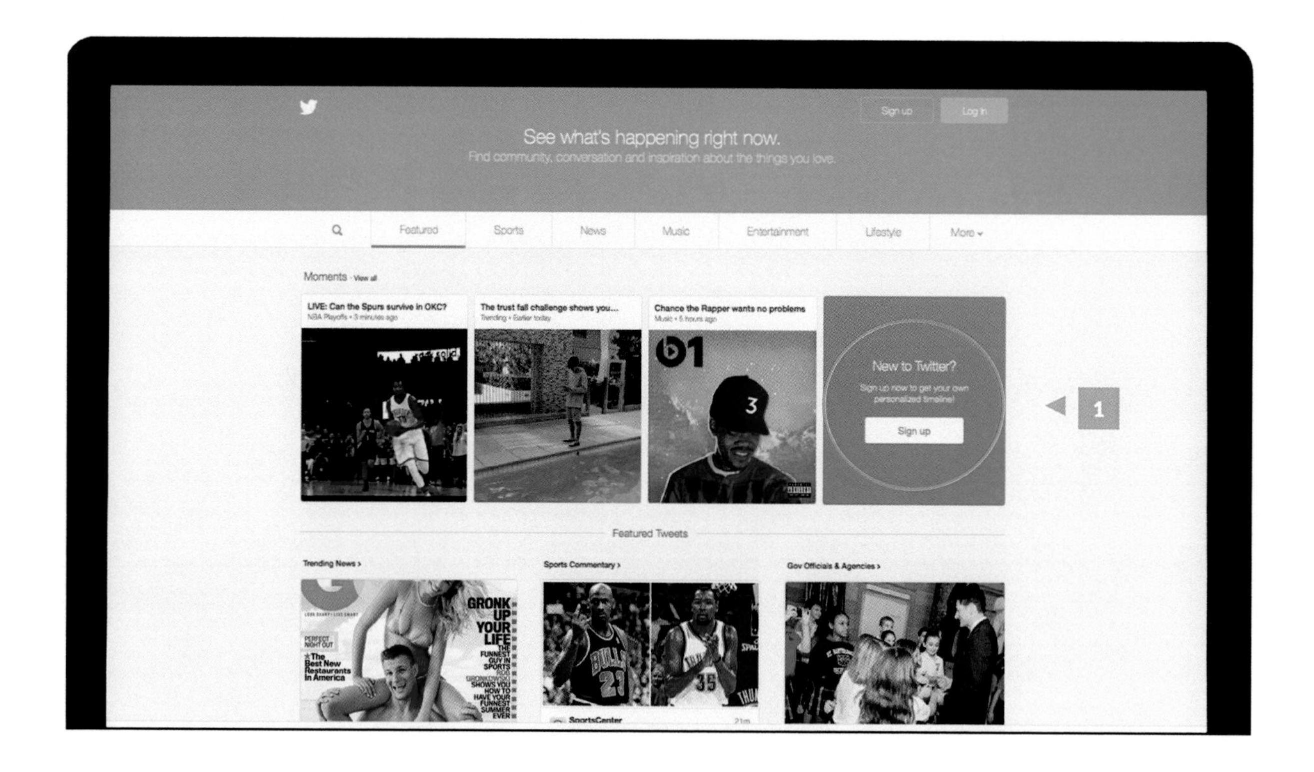

1

VISIT TWITTER.COM

Go directly to the website to begin the process of joining. It is free and you can sign up either on a computer or directly on your smart phone. It is beneficial to sign up on your smart phone - more on that later!

1. CREATE ACCOUNT You will see a large box that allows you to sign up if you are new. Click the "Sign up" button to get started.

2. CONTACT INFO You will need to provide a few pieces of information in order to join. The information you give here is just to set up your account and will not be visible to other users. The name you enter here is not the handle that will be used for "tweeting." That comes a bit later.

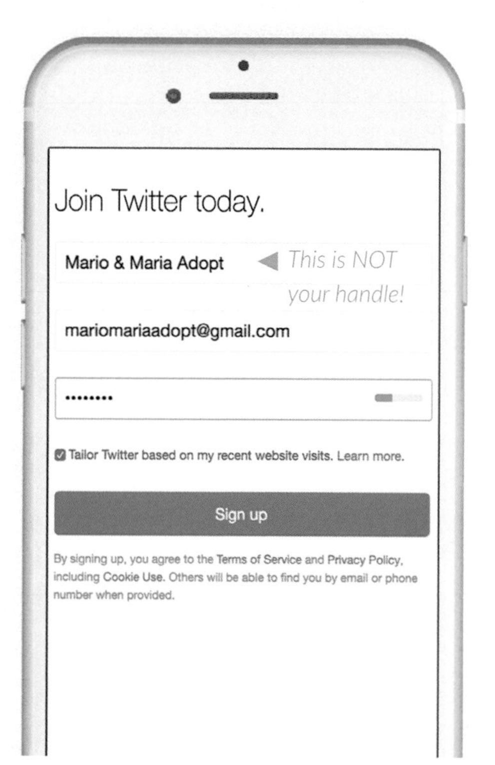

2

NOTE: *Twitter will use the email address you provide here to import your contacts (this is optional) so you may prefer using your personal email address rather than your new adoption-specific email address.*

3. ADD INTERESTS Twitter wants to know what you are interested in so it can show you people, organizations or businesses that you may want to follow. This is where you can search for both adoption-related and non-adoption related interests. Remember that what you enter here will help Twitter suggest relevant accounts for you to follow. It will also help Twitter suggest YOUR account to others which is key to creating a wider audience!

3 ▶

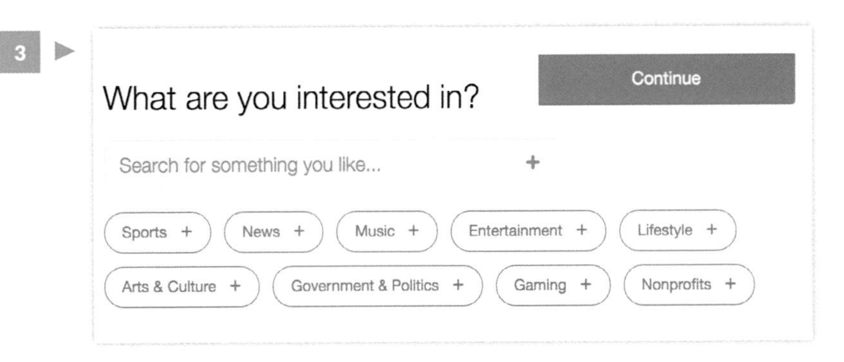

4. FIND FRIENDS You can import your email contacts and Twitter will use those email addresses to find people you know. This is NOT a way of inviting them to follow your newly created Twitter account, it will only show you which of your friends are on Twitter. If you are not interested in importing contacts or following your friends right now, you can easily skip this by clicking the "Skip for now" button.

By connecting with your phone number, you will sync your personal contacts, email contacts and Facebook contacts if you have these contacts synced to your phone already. This gives you the option to widen your audience/followers.

4 ▶

5. FOLLOW OTHERS Much like Facebook, Twitter curates a timeline full of people who are sharing tweets and photos. To create your timeline you need to start following other Twitter users. Twitter will suggest accounts to follow and as you begin following adoption-related accounts, it will suggest other adoption-related accounts you might find interesting. This is a great way to get your feet wet and you can follow other accounts as you go!

5 ▶

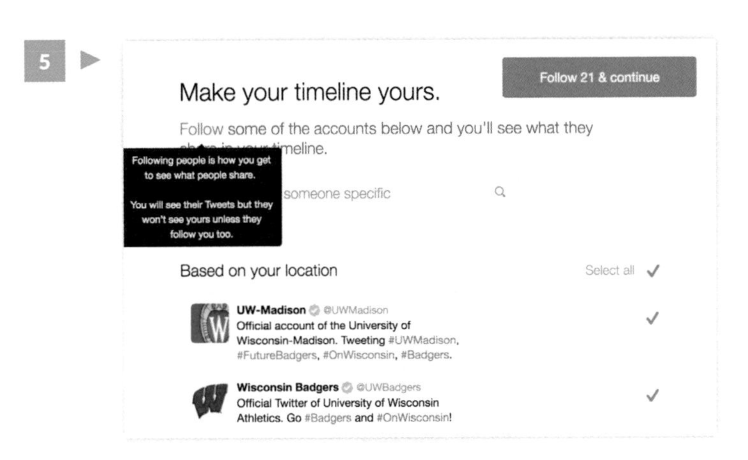

6. CREATE A HANDLE During the setup of your account, you will need to choose a username or handle. This name is limited to 15 characters and will be your Twitter identity. Every handle is unique and cannot be duplicated. Try to use a name as close to your branding as possible. If the name you want is not available, Twitter will show you suggestions that are close to your original name and still available to use.

6 ▶

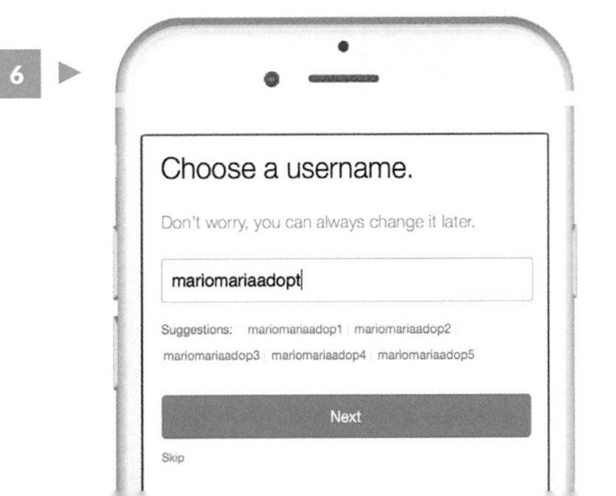

TWITTER

How to start using your Twitter account.

WELCOME TO TWITTER! *Now that your account is all set up, it's time to start building your network and, of course, tweeting! To maximize your outreach, you want to make sure you are using Twitter in the best way possible. Let's take a closer look on how to do just that!*

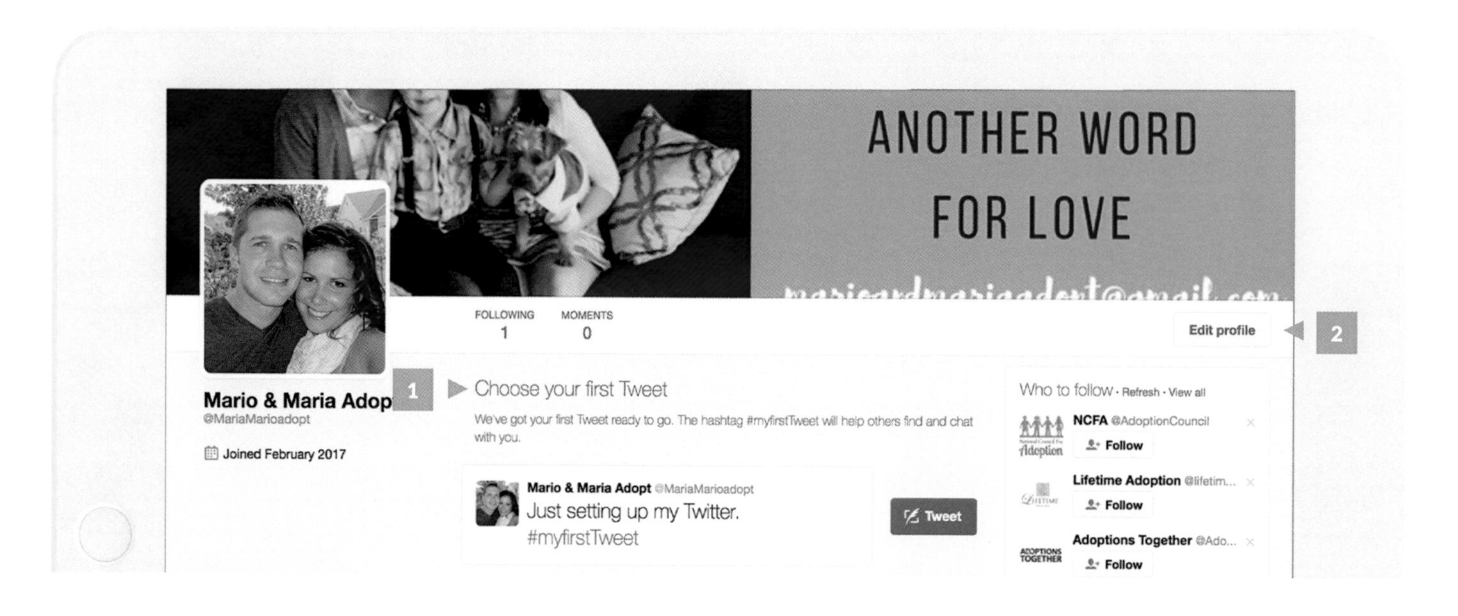

1. BEGIN TWEETING Once you have your account set up, you can begin tweeting! Tweets are short messages that can share stories (and photos,) ask questions to your followers, etc. You only have 140 characters to use in your tweets so be concise!

2. EDIT PROFILE If you want to make changes to your profile, add or change profile photos etc., you can do that easily by clicking on the "Edit Profile" button on the profile page of your account. This will bring you to the screen where you can make changes. When you are done, be sure to click the "Save changes" button.

3. FOLLOWING OTHERS It's a great idea to create a network on Twitter by following other users. Consider following other adoptive families to see how they are using Twitter for outreach. It's quite common if you follow someone, that they will follow you in return.

NOTE: *Twitter gives you the option to toggle back and forth between your personal account and your adoption twitter account.*

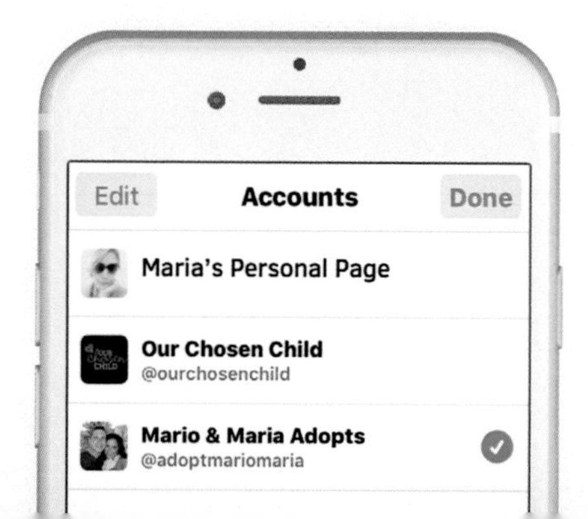

TWITTER

How to set up the perfect post in Twitter.

TWITTER

FORMAT

You have 140 characters to play with (for now) but that doesn't mean you should sacrifice grammar or spelling. Keep it short and snappy to get the most out of your content.

MENTIONS

If you're @mentioning someone at the beginning of a tweet, make sure to include a '.' before the @ - only accounts who follow both of you will be able to see it otherwise!

URLS

Depending on your tracking methods you can either Bitly your links – or just leave them as they are. Twitter cuts off links after a few characters so you don't need to worry about your tweet looking messy.

MESSAGE

LINK

LIVE FEEDS

Apps like Periscope and Meerkat make it possible for you to livestream events directly to your feed. It's less high maintenance than Facebook Live and allows you to just let it run in a high activity area of an event etc.

IMAGES

Use images to drive engagement alongside your tweet copy. To optimise for the platform resize to 1280x720.

VIDEOS

Upload your video files directly to the back end to get your creations to play directly in the feed! This is far more engaging than using a YouTube link.

REPLY · RETWEET · LIKE

SHARING

Share content from other accounts that is relevant to your followers. Don't forget to leave 20 characters so people can add their own content.

POLLS

Polls are a great tool for getting to know your followers – plus they're easy and quick to engage with, making it convenient for your followers to get involved.

SOURCE

GRAPHIC PROVIDED BY MY CLEVER AGENCY IN THEIR BLOG ON HOW TO CREATE PERFECT POSTS.

MYCLEVERAGENCY.COM/BLOG/2016/07/CREATE-PERFECT-POSTS-6-INFOGRAPHIC/

TWITTER

Tips for using Twitter for adoption outreach.

NOW THAT YOU ARE LIVE, ***let's take a look at some ideas to help you get the most out of using Twitter for your adoption outreach. How can you expand your network? What should you tweet about? How can you let others know you're on Twitter? Let's go over all of that and more!***

- Ensure that your entire Twitter profile is filled out including the two profile photos (profile and header), information in your bio and links to your webpage.

- Create a digital network on Twitter to communicate via tweeting and sharing photos and links. Since the network you create reflects on you and your adoption journey, choose whom you follow carefully to build a positive, adoption-centric community.

- Share your Twitter username on other forms of social media to gain more followers. For example, Hopefully Parents' Twitter username in a post looks like this: "Follow me at @hopefullyparents."

- Search for groups and interests that are similar to yours. Once you follow them, you can curate their content by retweeting their tweets.

- Use attention-grabbing titles for Twitter posts such as "How to..." or "Contact us for..." or even "It's hard to believe, but..."

- Do not try to follow everyone! It seems like a great idea but choosing meaningful followers is more important for gaining meaningful connections. Every person you are connected with will see your posts, so ensure that you are comfortable with the followers you have.

- When it comes to tweeting, more really is merrier! Use a Twitter application to schedule multiple tweets so they go out several times a day.

- Tweeting during peak times will increase the number of people that are engaging with your posts. The best time to tweet is between 1 PM and 3 PM, your local time. The worst time is between 8 PM and 8 AM.

NOTE: *For more information on peak times to use popular social media platforms, see page 98.*

- Look into interesting or trending topics and retweet them or generate your own posts using trending hashtags.

- Be brand-consistent by using keywords as hashtags and by using your most important hashtags on all your posts. See the example from Chris and Troy below:

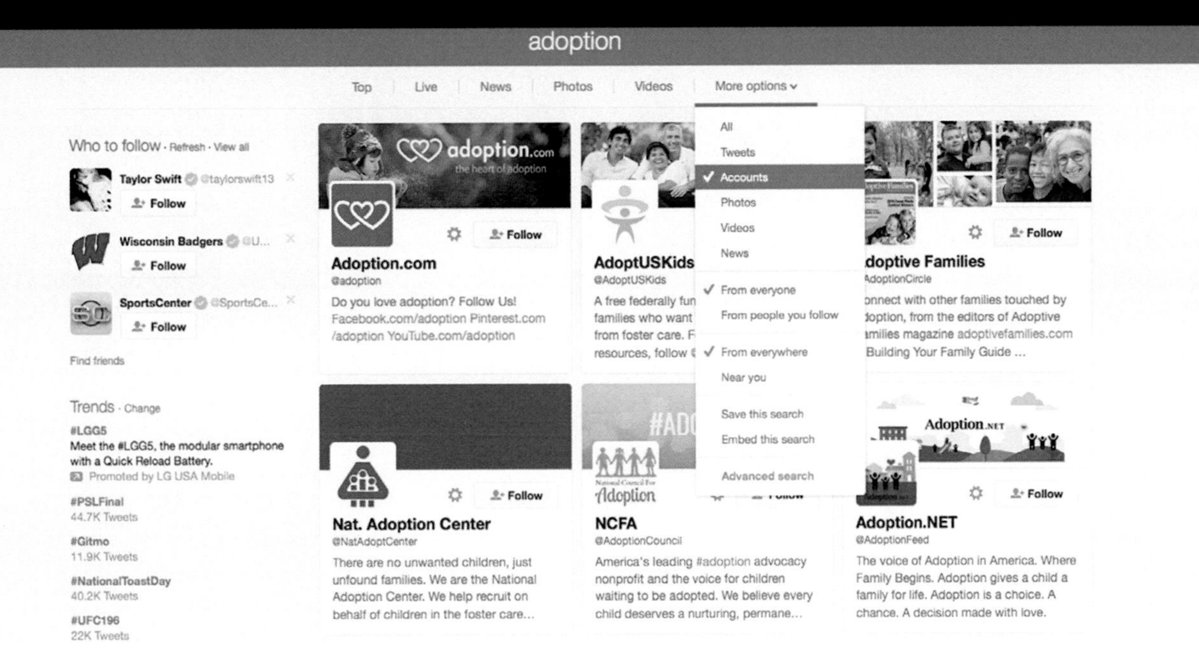

▲ SEARCHES

To expand your connections within the adoption community on Twitter, you can do searches for specific topics such as open adoption, domestic adoption, etc. You will find other resources available and you can follow their tweets. This is a great way to expand your network and connect with other users.

◀ CONNECTING TO CONTACTS

Just like other social media platforms, you can let your contacts know that you are now on Twitter by easily linking your Twitter account with your Facebook adoption account. That way anything you post on Twitter will automatically show up on your Facebook page as well. It's a great way to double your networking at one time!

ADD LINKS TO YOUR BLOG OR WEBSITE IN YOUR BIO THEN USE THE HASHTAG #LINKINBIO. THAT WAY YOU CAN PROMOTE YOUR SITE OR BLOG WITHOUT USING UP YOUR 140 CHARACTER LIMIT.

INSTAGRAM

How to set up an Instagram account.

YOU MIGHT BE WONDERING ***what's all the fuss about Instagram and how is it different from Facebook or Twitter? Good question! Instagram is a photo and video based app. It is much more visual than Facebook since posts are only (and always!) photos or videos. You may post text as a comment to your photo but the main content is the photo. For Instagram, hashtags are key to discovering new content and, more importantly, to being discovered!***

GETTING STARTED

This is not an application that you can use solely from a computer. You can set up an account, view your feed and like posts from your computer, but you must use your phone or a tablet to post on Instagram. You will need to go to the Apple Store or Google Play and download Instagram to your smart phone or tablet in order to post and share photos or videos.

CONTACT INFO

You will need to provide a phone number and/or email to sign up. While you can do either, we suggest using your cell phone number to create an account. When you sign up with your phone number, you will have the opportunity to select contacts on your phone (from email and other social media accounts) and choose to follow them if they are also on Instagram.

SET UP AN INSTAGRAM ACCOUNT

1. CREATE ACCOUNT You can sign up for an account using a computer (see example below) or you can sign up on your phone/tablet once you download the application. It's up to you!

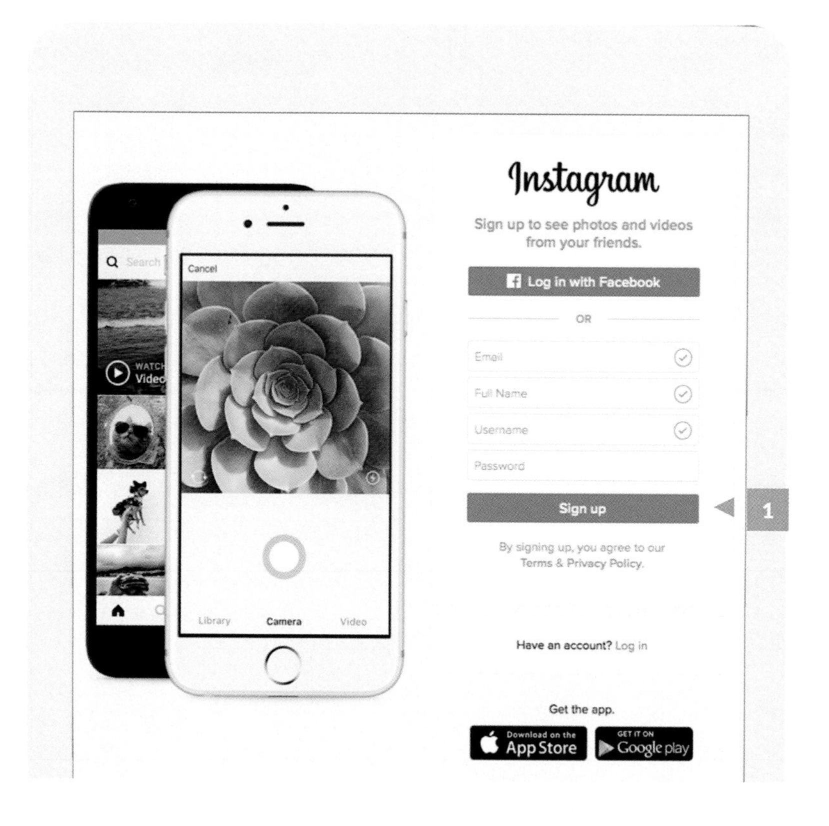

WHY USE INSTAGRAM?

- Most people are drawn to photos over text so this is the place to share lots of creative and unique photos to capture interest and gain a wider audience.
- It is really easy to link to Facebook to increase your followers and post to both applications at the same time.
- Instagram is free and fun to use! If you already use Instagram personally, it is simple to toggle between accounts for personal use and adoption outreach.
- Instagram captures a younger demographic than Facebook, so it makes sense to use both for your outreach.

2. SET UP YOUR PROFILE Now that you have signed up for an account, it is time to fill in the details of your profile. This is the very next screen you will see after starting your account

If you already have an Instagram account, you can easily add a new account for adoption outreach. Simply go to your existing profile, click on the "gear" symbol in the top right corner and scroll down to "Add Account." Click on this and follow the instructions to create your new account!

3. NEEDED INFORMATION The four items listed beneath your profile photo will be publicly shown anytime someone looks at your profile. Feel free to enter in your website, Hopefully Parents page, blog or Facebook page in the website line. We recommend sharing your adoption-specific contact information here.

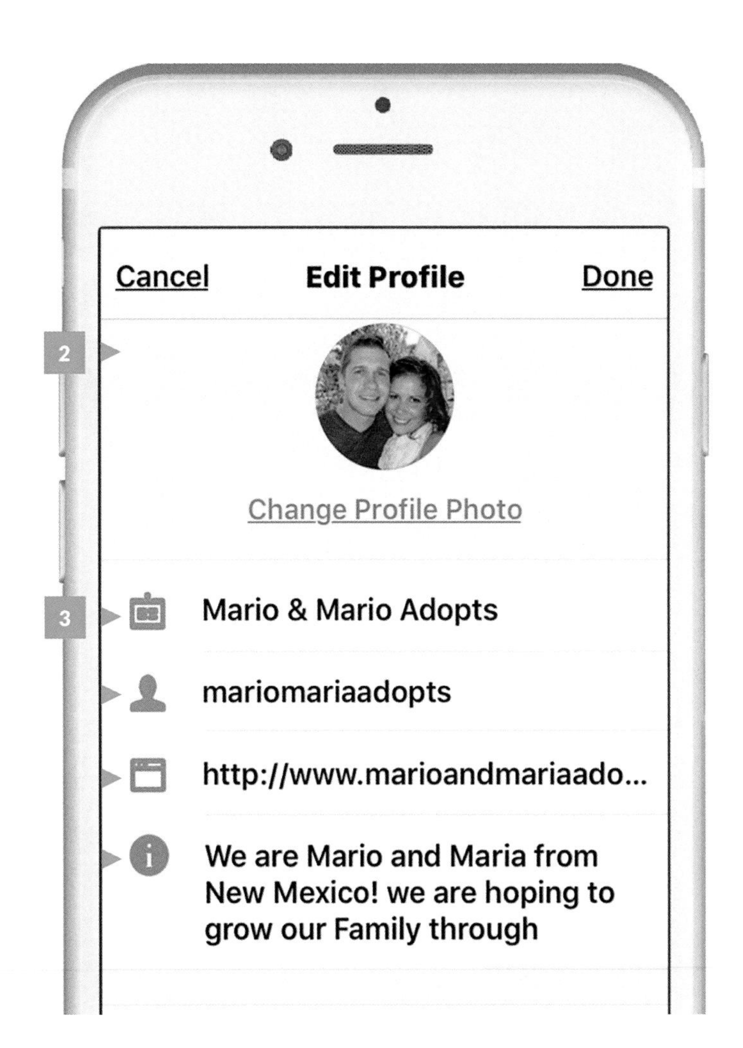

▼ *Learn about the Instagram menu bar*

START BUILDING

FIND PEOPLE TO FOLLOW

Now that your account is active, you can start finding other people to follow to build your feed. You can search for particular people or topics that interest you. Once you locate someone, click on their profile and press the "Follow" button. This way, anything they share will show up in your feed.

USE HASHTAGS

You can also search using hashtags and see what results Instagram finds for you. This can be a great way to find new ideas and new people to follow! Try searching #adoptionrocks and get connected with the vibrant adoption community on Instagram!

NOTE: *See page 86 for some great adoption-related hashtag examples.*

MENU BAR

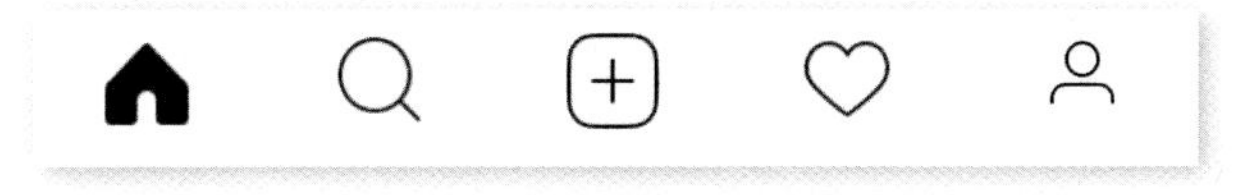

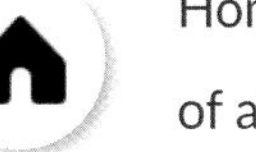

Home - this will take you to the news feed of all the new things shared.

Search - this is how to look up a certain person, topic or hashtag.

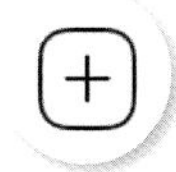

Add - if you want to share a photo or video, this is where you can add it.

Like - this will show you people who "like" and comment on your posts.

Profile - if you want to go directly to your profile and make changes, click here.

INSTAGRAM

How to start using your Instagram account.

IF YOU'RE NEW TO INSTAGRAM ***you are in for a treat! Instagram is a great way to connect with people whom share your common interests, like adoption! There is a vibrant and active adoption community on Instagram so, in addition to using Instagram for outreach, you will find a welcoming and supportive community too. Getting active on Instagram is easy and fun. Let's walk through the initial steps now!***

TAKING PHOTOS

To share a picture, click on the "+" button at the bottom of your screen. (see below)

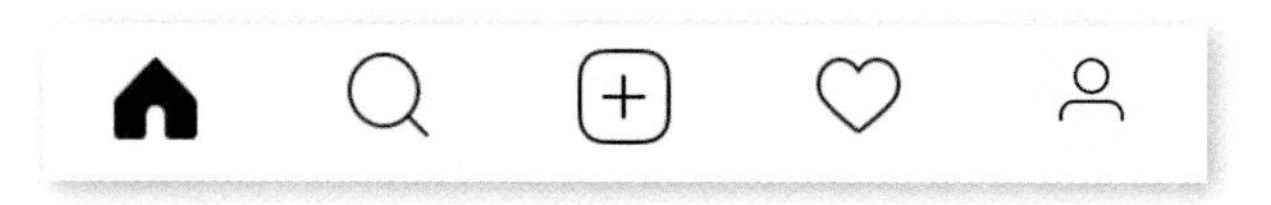

This will open up your camera in order to take a picture. If this is your first time using Instagram, you might get a box asking permission to access your camera. Go ahead and click "OK." Next, focus in on what you want to capture and then click the large, round button.

This will flip the screen so the camera is facing you. Hint: Selfies!

This will turn the flash on or off.

1. LIBRARY You can also use photos or videos stored on your phone if you click on the "Library" button. It is sometimes more convenient to take a photo and store it for posting later, when you have more time to upload your photo, write your caption and include your hashtags.

This allows you to select multiple photos for one post. It's a great way to post a selection of photos. Your audience will be able to scroll through and see each photo!

2. VIDEO If you want to made a video and share it, click on the "Video" button.

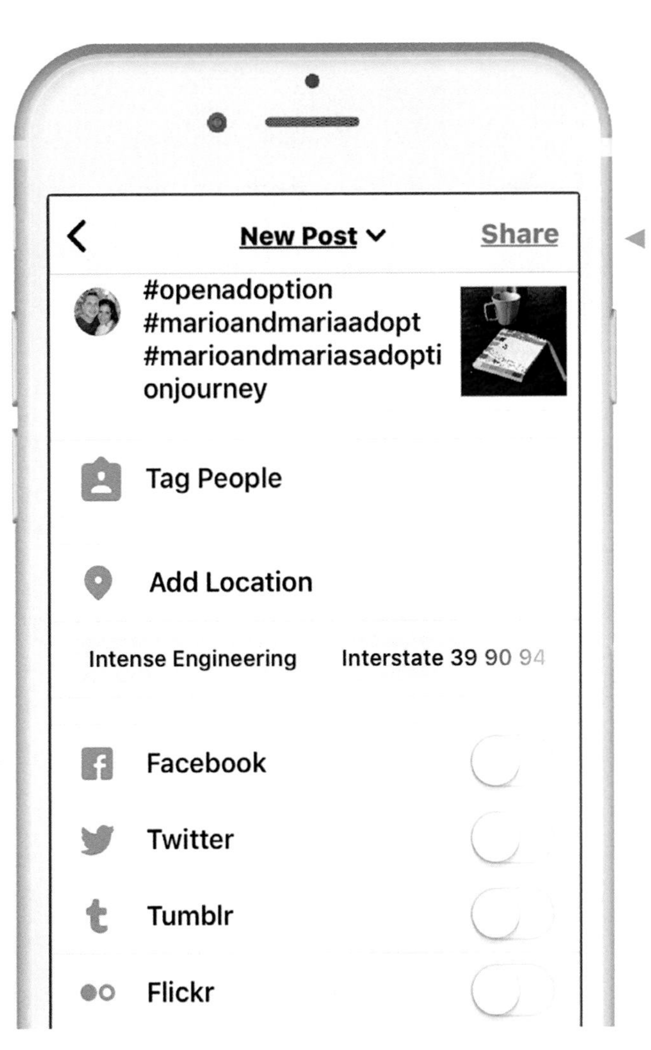

3. USE A FILTER! Photo filters are integrated in the Instagram app. They are fun ways to enhance photos slightly or make them really artistic or creative. You can click on any filter and it will show you the effect on your photo right away. If you don't want to use a filter, just click on the "Normal" setting. Have fun playing with them and making your photos pop!

4. WRITE A CAPTION You have the option to write a caption to your photo. It will appear at the top of the comments section rather than as a heading or a caption directly under your image. After you write your caption, you can include your hashtags. For more information on how to properly format your caption and hashtags, see the next page.

5. TAG PEOPLE If you are sharing a photo and you want to tag someone else or multiple people, you can click on this spot to add them.

6. ADD LOCATION This is where you can add the location for the picture that you are sharing. Are you somewhere really cool like Disneyland? Are you just hanging out at home? Feel free to click here and add your location.

NOTE! When you tag others or add a location to your post, this acts much like a hashtag. Meaning, when someone searches for the location or person you tagged, your post will be shown. This is a great way to gain exposure!

7. SHARING ON OTHER SITES If you have other social media accounts linked to Instagram, this is where you can share the same photo on the other sites as well. Slide the button on any linked account listed to share your photo there simultaneously. We highly encourage this!

8. CLICK THE SHARE BUTTON This will officially post your picture on Instagram!

INSTAGRAM

Popular hashtags and using them in Instagram.

POPULAR HASHTAGS ***Here are some examples of different hashtags related to adoption that you can use!***

- #adopt
- #adoption
- #adoptionisawesome
- #adoptionisbeautiful
- #adoptionislove
- #adoptionjourney
- #adoptionoutreach
- #adoptionprofile
- #adoptionrocks
- #adoptivefamilies
- #adoptivefamily
- #birthmother
- #buildingfamilies
- #domesticadoption
- #familyiseverything
- #hopefuladoptivefamily
- #hopefuladoptiveparents
- #hopingtoadopt
- #hopingtobeparents
- #lovemakesafamily
- #openadoption
- #parentprofile
- #prospectiveadoptiveparents
- #waitingfamilies
- #waitingfamily
- #worththewait

LINK SOCIAL MEDIA ACCOUNTS

When you share a photo or video on Instagram, it can also post directly on your Facebook community page, Twitter account or on other social media accounts. We highly recommend linking your social media accounts together so that anything you share will be seen in multiple places.

To link accounts, go to your profile and click the "settings" symbol in the upper right corner. Scroll down to "Linked Accounts" and click on any application that you want to link. Instagram will walk you through the process of connecting the two accounts.

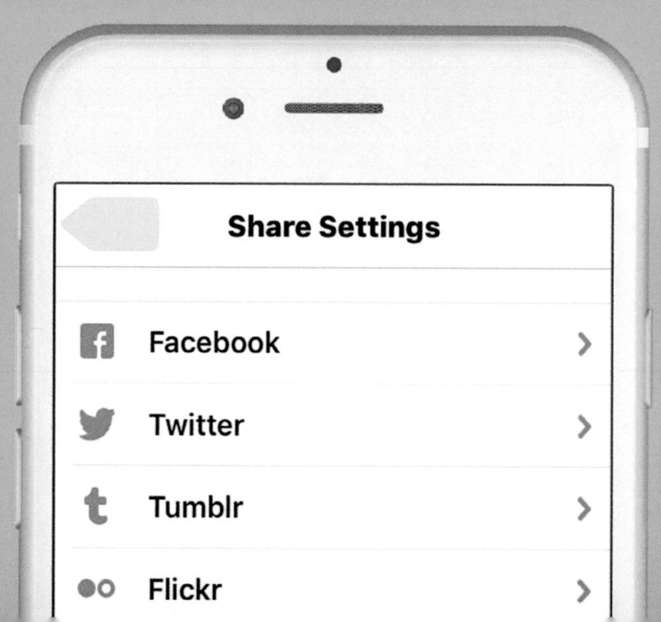

INSTAGRAM

How to set up the perfect post in Instagram.

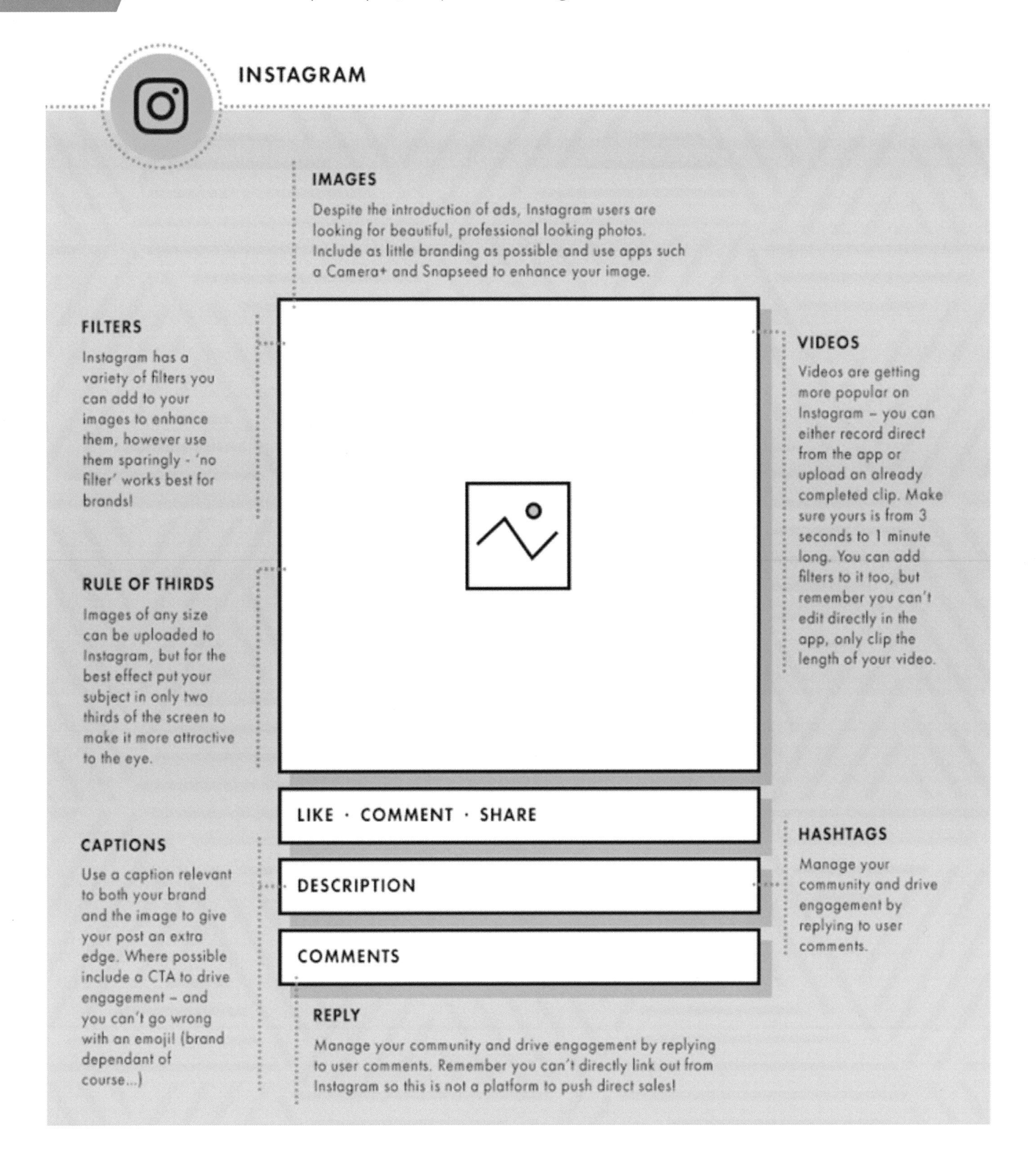

SOURCE

GRAPHIC PROVIDED BY MY CLEVER AGENCY IN THEIR BLOG ON HOW TO CREATE PERFECT POSTS.

MYCLEVERAGENCY.COM/BLOG/2016/07/CREATE-PERFECT-POSTS-6-INFOGRAPHIC/

INSTAGRAM

Tips on using Instagram for adoption outreach.

NOW THAT YOUR ACCOUNT IS ACTIVE, ***it is time to make it work for you and your adoption outreach! You can share all kinds of things like a nursery that you might be working on, a bike trail near your home that you enjoy using, what you're cooking for dinner or a get together of family and friends. Have fun trying new filters and sharing a window into your life. Be real and be sure to proofread!***

- To gain followers, make sure to be active user on Instagram by "liking" and commenting on other people's photos and by following others. Research has shown that for every 100 random likes you give to photos, you will gain about 6 new followers.
- Add a direct link from your Instagram profile to your website or blog.
- Increase followers by adding Facebook friends and email contacts.
- Be brand consistent by using your keywords as hashtags and by using the same hashtags everytime you post a photo or video.
- Check your image size to make sure you aren't cropping things out of your photo that you want to include. Make sure to also include personalized text along with your keywords on pictures that you share.
- Discover new or different hashtags to use for your posts by searching for other adoption related pages that fit in well with your brand.
- Be sure to find other people that you want to follow. Choosing different people to follow can lead to new connections and new ideas.
- Discover if others are also using your hashtag to describe their photos. If too many people are using the same hashtag, reword the phrase to narrow the number of posts an audience will see.
- Decide if the hashtags you have been using are supporting your brand and representing your images well; if not, just rework the hashtag to fit better with your keywords.

Maria is accomplishing all of these things with her post:

√ Engaging her audience with something fun to look at.

√ Giving people a chance to know more about her hobby of cardmaking.

√ Using hashtags every time she posts for greater branding.

√ Posting things about her daily life and who she is.

CLIENT INTERVIEW

An interview with Brent and Heather about Instagram.

THE FOLLOWING INFORMATION *is from an interview with Brent and Heather. Heather is an adoptive mom who really took to Instagram and used that as her primary social media platform. She has built a large and dedicated following within the adoption community. Here are some insights and guidance from her!*

WHY DID YOU CHOOSE INSTAGRAM FOR YOUR ADOPTION OUTREACH?

I found Instagram as the best social media outlet for adoption outreach because it was the easiest and best option for what I needed most during the beginning stages of adoption and during the dreadful wait: community, hope and visual proof. I found the use of searching hashtags (#adoptionrocks #lovemakesafamily #adoptionbuiltus) helped me easily find a community of other adoptive parents at different stages of the process with whom I could connect. Seeing the pictures of the daily lives of parents with their child/children helped me see just how beautiful the end result of the adoption process is, which helped me get through the tough stuff.

WHY DID YOU USE YOUR HASHTAGS WHEN POSTING ON INSTAGRAM?

Hashtags were my ticket to community. By using common adoption hashtags, I did and continue to find other adoptive families to connect with. I hope that, by continuing to use these hashtags, other people who might be exploring adoption as an option or other adoptive families can find my feed and, hopefully, I can provide them the hope and encouragement others gave me during the trials and tribulations I encountered on the long road to our daughter Willa.

HEATHER AND BRENT WITH THEIR ADORABLE BABY GIRL, WILLA

DID ANY EXPECTANT PARENTS REACH OUT TO YOU FROM YOUR POSTS?

Yes, but none of those situations came to fruition. In the end, we matched and placed through our agency.

ANY ADVICE FOR THOSE IN THEIR ADOPTION JOURNEY?

Adoption is hard. It requires incredible faith and sacrifice. There are definitely days when it all feels heavy and hard to carry and it's easy to wonder if it's worth it all. Let me tell you this: There is nothing more worth it. I believe my Willa, her life, and our road to her is the most beautiful love story to have ever been written. I would go through all of the hard work over and over and over again if it means I get to be her mama. Adoption is amazing and I feel incredibly blessed that I was called as one of the lucky few who get to experience it; you will too, I promise!

INSTAGRAM

The finer points of using Instagram.

1. DIRECT MESSAGING VIA INSTAGRAM If someone wants to contact you in Instagram they can do that one of two ways. First, they can look in your bio for your contact info (as noted on page 82) or they can send you a Direct Message (DM).

   Instagram Direct is the messaging tool located in the top right corner of your Instagram feed. Direct messaging is a private way to connect and send messages to other people on Instagram.

2. CREATING INSTAGRAM STORIES
   With the "Stories" feature you can share a video that is only available for 24 hours. It does not post to your news feed but allows any of your followers the chance to view it. If anyone that you are following shares a story, you will find those at the top of your news feed. These are becoming more and more popular!

   Just note that this is a raw, unedited video. You can not create a story, tweak it and then post it. If you want an edited video, you can create one outside of Instagram and then share it on your profile.

   NOTE! *When you post a story, your followers are able to comment at the bottom in the form of a message. If you receive a comment on your story it will show up in your Direct Message box as a new message.*

3. ADDING "." TO YOUR POST
   You might have seen the use of periods in posts on Instagram and wondered, "Why or how do they do that?" Well, the answer to why is simple—to break up the text and create a much cleaner look when folks are looking at your posts. They can easily read just your caption or story yet the hashtags are still associated with the post for branding but not jumbled all together.

   So, how do you accomplish this? It's really simple! All you have to do is write out the message that goes with your picture or video. Once you have that finished, press "return" and then "." and then repeat those steps a few times to put in a few lines of periods. After that you can list all the hashtags you want to use and then post your new image or video.

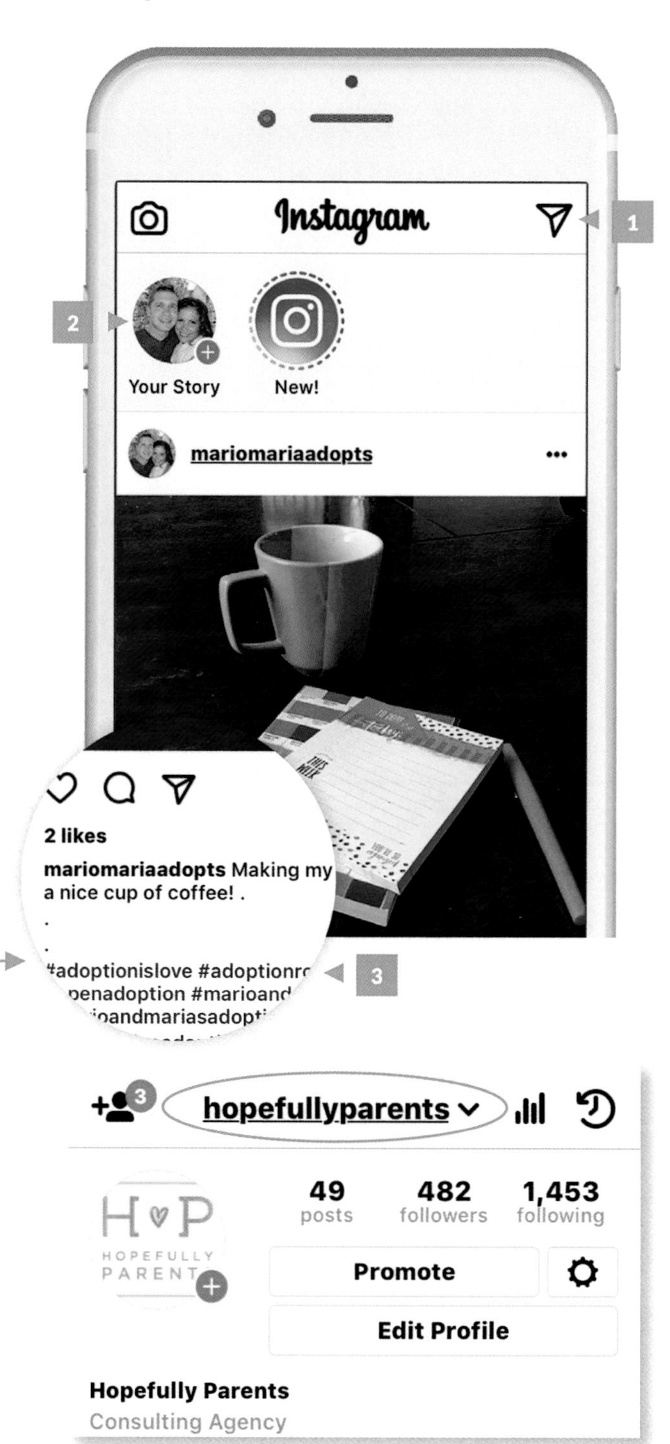

▲ *If you have created an account just for adoption outreach, in addition to a personal or business account, you can easily toggle between the different accounts by going to your profile page and clicking on your account name.*

CLIENT INTERVIEW

An interview with Josh and Jessica about Instagram.

WE ARE GRATEFUL FOR *another family sharing their experience and thoughts about using Instagram for their adoption outreach. In this interview, Jessica talks about the way they used their Instagram account more for support and networking than actively trying to match with an expectant family. They have a huge Instagram following and are active in the adoption community.*

WHY DID YOU CHOOSE INSTAGRAM FOR YOUR ADOPTION OUTREACH?

Originally I created our adoption Instagram account (@thecunhasadoptionjourney) for support and to meet families who were on the same journey as us.

WHY DID YOU USE HASHTAGS WHEN POSTING ON INSTAGRAM?

I used hashtags so potential birth mothers and birth fathers could find us and so they could get to know us on a more personal level. I didn't want to only use our profile as a means to get to know us. My Instagram page is me also (well, us but I run it. My husband isn't big on social media.) I'm very open with our journey. And lastly, so families that were on the same journey as us could find us and relate, ask questions and know they are not alone.

DID ANY POTENTIAL EXPECTANT PARENTS REACH OUT TO YOU FROM YOUR POSTS?

Yes. I had one potential birth mother contact me, via DM. She was sweet and we became "social media friends," as we have never met in person.

WHAT HAS BEEN YOUR FAVORITE PART OF SHARING YOUR JOURNEY?

The best part is all the amazing families I have "met" along the way and all the birth mothers that I have "met." I get

JESSICA AND JOSH MATCHED AND NOW HAVE A SON, PICTURED ABOVE

DM's all the time from families who are waiting for that call and they tell me that they have been following our journey since the beginning and it gives them hope. And birth mothers tell me that when they see pictures of my son, it's a reminder about how happy their birth child is and how happy they feel to have made a family.

DO YOU HAVE ANY OTHER ADVICE FOR THOSE IN THEIR ADOPTION JOURNEY?

Never give up. Never lose faith. When you are having a bad day, which you will, just know that your baby is out there. He or she may not be born yet, but they are out there. And I promise you, promise, promise, promise, the wait is absolutely worth it.

PINTEREST

How to set up an account on Pinterest.

PINTEREST IS A FAST-GROWING *site where people can share ideas and inspiration about any topic and save ideas on organized boards. It is also a way to store and then share all of the fun ideas that you encounter on the Internet, like a digital bulletin board. This is a great tool to use in your adoption journey. You can gather all sorts of ideas for your adoption outreach and begin planning your future as a family. Let's see how it works!*

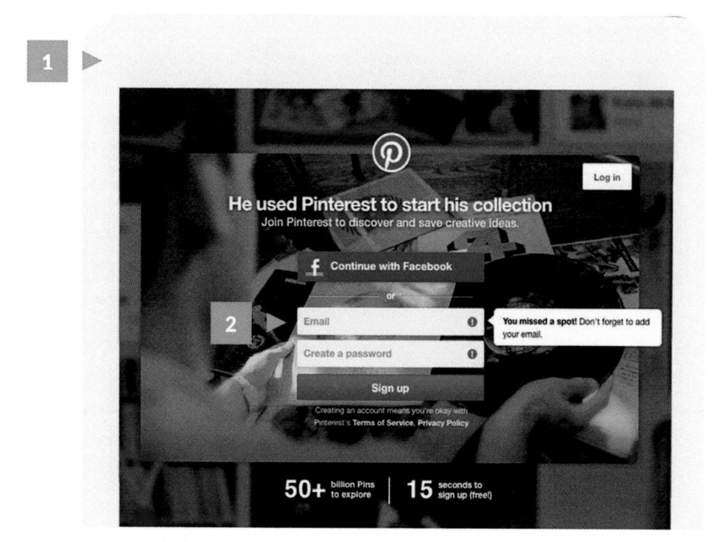

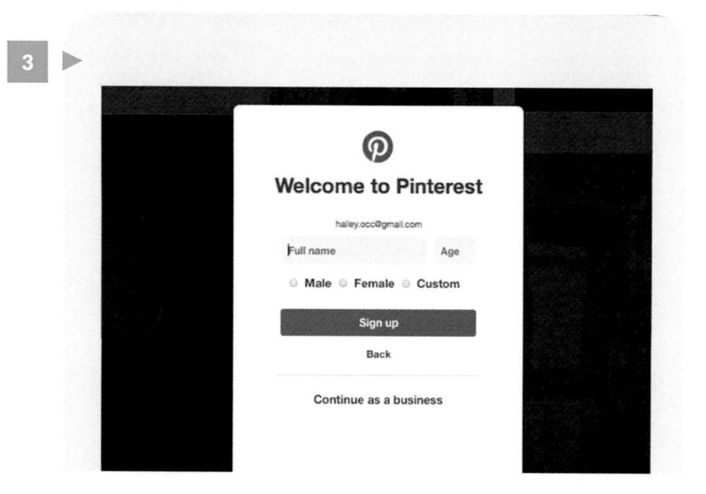

SET UP AN ACCOUNT ON PINTEREST

1. VISIT PINTEREST.COM Go directly to the Pinterest website to create your account. You can do this on your phone or computer.

2. ENTER EMAIL AND PASSWORD Enter an email address that will be associated with this Pinterest account. This email address will not be visible to the public. We recommend using your personal email address so you are able to import your contacts.

3. SIGN UP Like with other social media accounts your "name" on Pinterest should be consistent and relate to your adoption journey. Your account name will be shown publicly both on your page and on your pins. As people re-pin your pins on their own boards, your name will stay associated with the pin and that is great for your visibility!

4. FOLLOW 5 TOPICS Pinterest wants to know what you are interested in so they can show you topics and images that relate to your interests in your home feed. These can be adoption-related or can relate to your hobbies and interests.

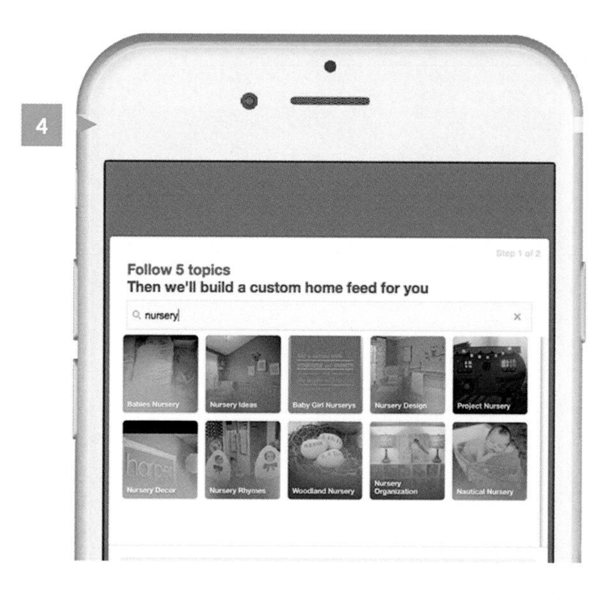

HELPFUL HINT

YOU CAN (AND SHOULD) LINK PINTEREST TO YOUR ADOPTION FACEBOOK PAGE.

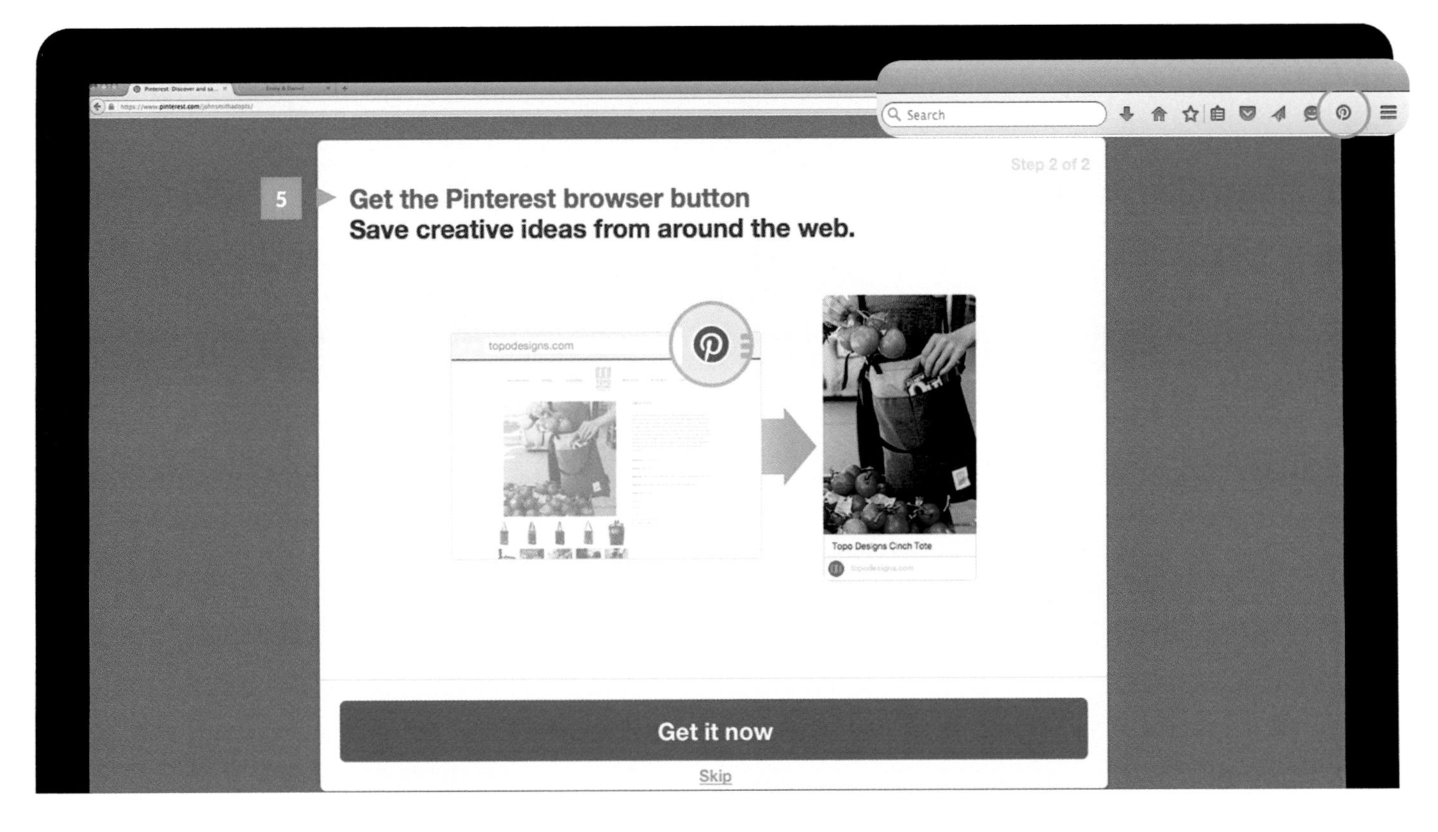

5. BROWSER BUTTON If you want to be able to use a Pinterest button, this is how you set it up (and you can do it at any time). It puts a little Pinterest button up on your Internet toolbar. Then, when you are on a website and want to "pin" it to Pinterest, all you have to do is click that little button, (see picture above). It comes in pretty handy!

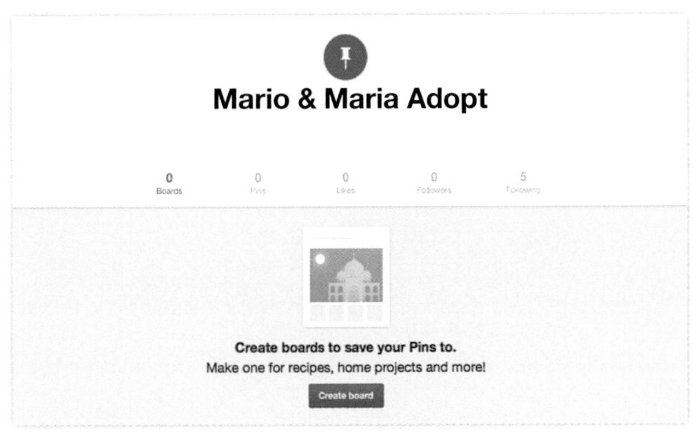

WELCOME TO PINTEREST!

Once you have created your account, it is time to start creating boards where you can post pins. These boards can be things like:

- Places we want to take our child
- Traveling adventures to conquer
- Recipes to try
- Nursery decor ideas
- Birthday party ideas
- Baby announcement ideas

NOTE! For more help on creating boards, see the very next page!

MENU BAR

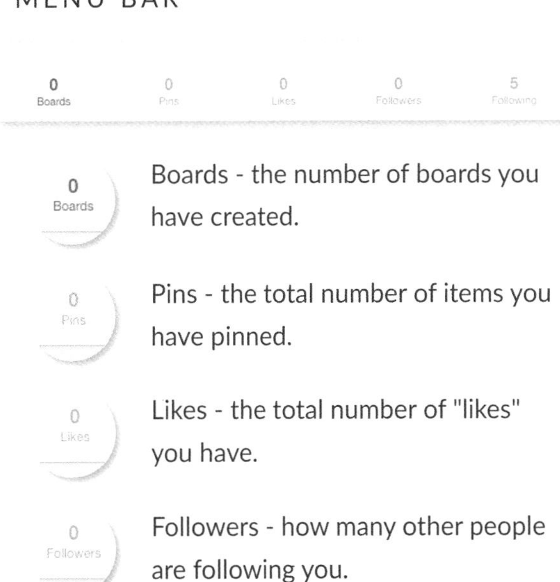

Boards - the number of boards you have created.

Pins - the total number of items you have pinned.

Likes - the total number of "likes" you have.

Followers - how many other people are following you.

Following - the number of people you are following.

PINTEREST

How to start using your Pinterest account.

NOW THAT YOUR ACCOUNT IS SET UP, ***let's start filling in details! Pinterest is different from the other social media platforms we have discussed in that it does not curate a chronological "newsfeed" with posts, but rather it provides a platform for you to create static "boards" full of pins (images) that others can browse. We'll walk you through the specifics below!***

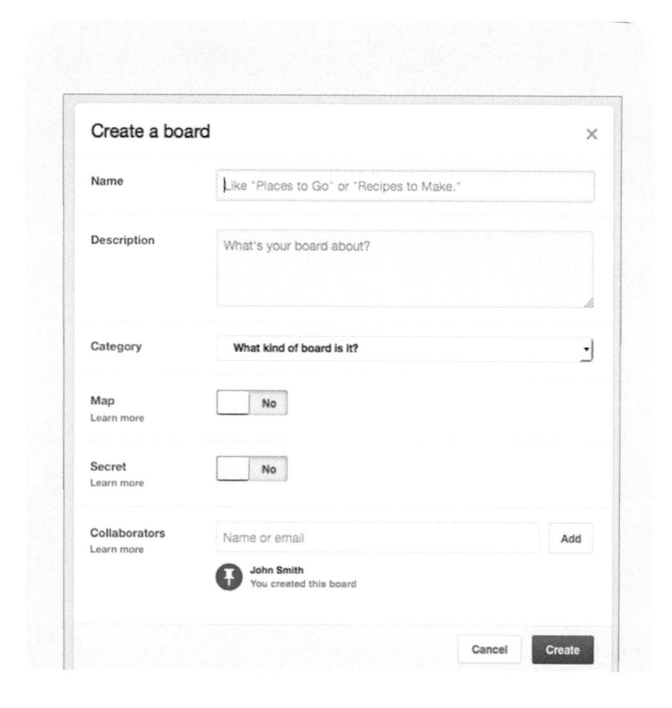

CREATE A BOARD

Boards can be as broad or specific as you want. You could have a board of dinner recipes (broad) or a board of new enchilada recipes (specific). Create a few to get started and think about what is most relevant to your adoption outreach. You can always add more boards as you go along.

If you are still a little stuck, you can do a search in Pinterest and look at other adoption boards or other waiting family boards to see what they look like. It might give you some inspiration, as well as someone new to follow!

Be descriptive when entering the details for your boards. Pinterest will search the descriptive text and suggest your boards to others searching for things you might have mentioned in your text.

PINNING

You can re-pin images you discover on other's boards, or you can pin original content you find other places on the internet. Websites with recipes, for instance, often have a "Pin It!" button that will save your favorites onto your boards. By curating interesting boards with lots of pins, you increase the chances that other pinners will browse your boards and re-pin your images. When they re-pin, your username (adoption-specific of course!) and comments go with the pin. This is a great way to gain visibility for your adoption outreach!

It's important to write interesting, descriptive captions for the items you pin. The captions should share your personality and, if possible, some insight into your adoption journey. A caption could be "These curtains are perfect for the nursery we are putting together for the child we hope to adopt someday!"

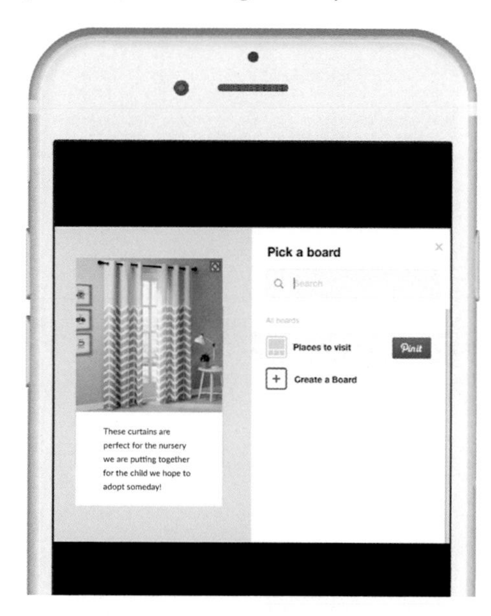

HELPFUL HINT

IT'S BETTER TO HAVE MORE BOARDS THAT ARE SPECIFIC IN PURPOSE RATHER THAN A SINGLE BOARD WITH A MISH-MASH OF PINS.

PINTEREST

How to set up the perfect post in Pinterest.

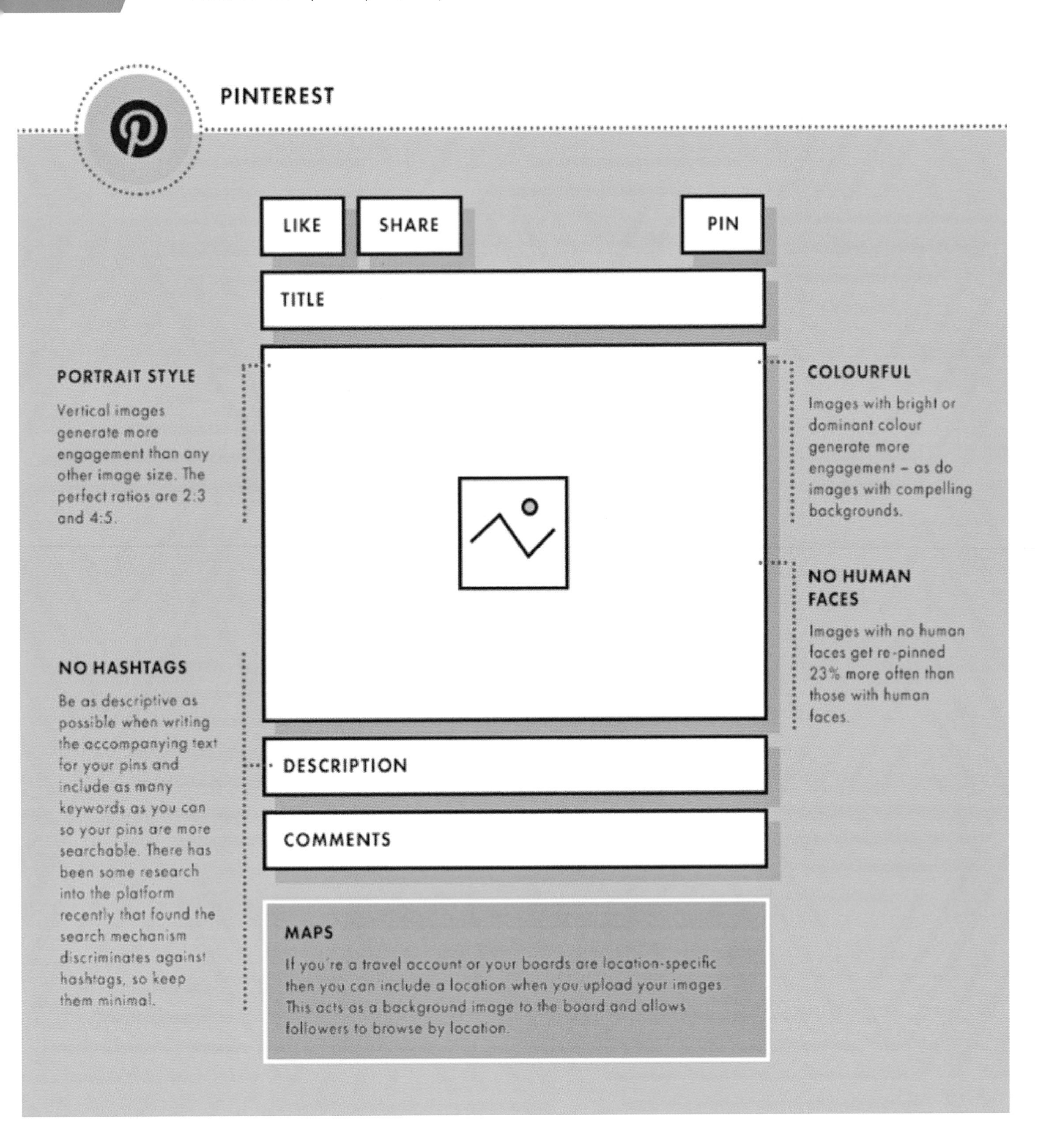

SOURCE

GRAPHIC PROVIDED BY MY CLEVER AGENCY IN THEIR BLOG ON HOW TO CREATE PERFECT POSTS.

MYCLEVERAGENCY.COM/BLOG/2016/07/CREATE-PERFECT-POSTS-6-INFOGRAPHIC/

PINTEREST

Tips on using Pinterest for adoption outreach.

SINCE YOUR GOAL ***is to use Pinterest for your adoption outreach, let's think about how to use Pinterest not only for fun, but also to connect you with expectant parents who may be considering adoption.***

- Choose a Pinterest profile image that will be a recognizable face or logo for your adoption brand.
- Connect your Pinterest page to your website and other social media pages through your settings.
- Add a description of your adoption journey, what this page means to you and of course, use your keywords.
- Invite your friends to follow your board! Your Pinterest profile settings tab will allow you to invite friends through email or your social media accounts.
- Add the 'Pin It' button to your website or blog. That way, if someone likes what you shared, they can easily "pin" your page or content to their boards. To add this, go to developers.pinterest.com/tools/widget-builder.
- A Pinterest page is a great way to express who you are and what you like through images that reflect your interests, hobbies and passions. It does not need to be entirely about your adoption journey but it should reflect who you are in a positive way, very much like your adoption profile.
- If someone re-pins something you have pinned, your original text and link will follow the pin onto their board. Because of this, each piece of content added to your page will need a description relating back to your adoption journey.

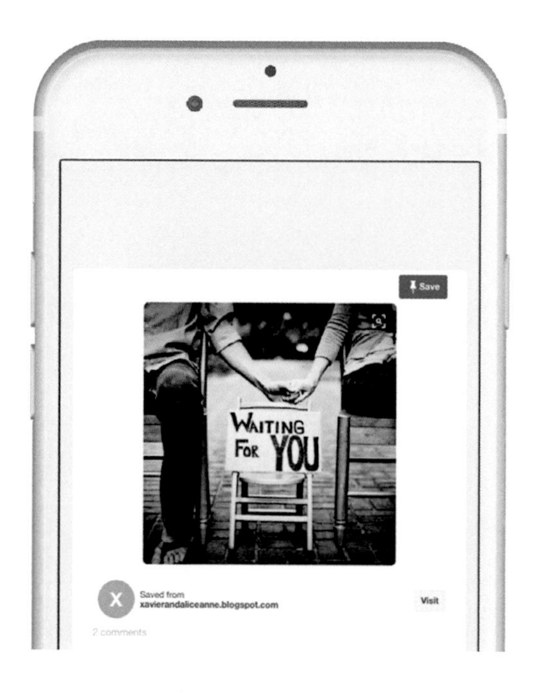

- Pinterest can be addictive! Have fun but stay focused on your adoption journey. Be disciplined about adding fun and relevant content. Make sure to add titles and comments that share your adoption social media accounts or your website/blog.
- Follow other friends and boards that relate to your adoption journey, keywords and brand. The more friends and followers you interact with, the larger network you can create.
- Always keep in mind that Pinterest is a place to discover content. Share things that will promote your boards and pages. It's important to stay current with your page so people will keep checking your content and spreading the word about your adoption journey.

HELPFUL HINT

MAKE SURE YOUR BOARDS ARE SET TO "PUBLIC" SO THEY CAN BE EASILY DISCOVERED!

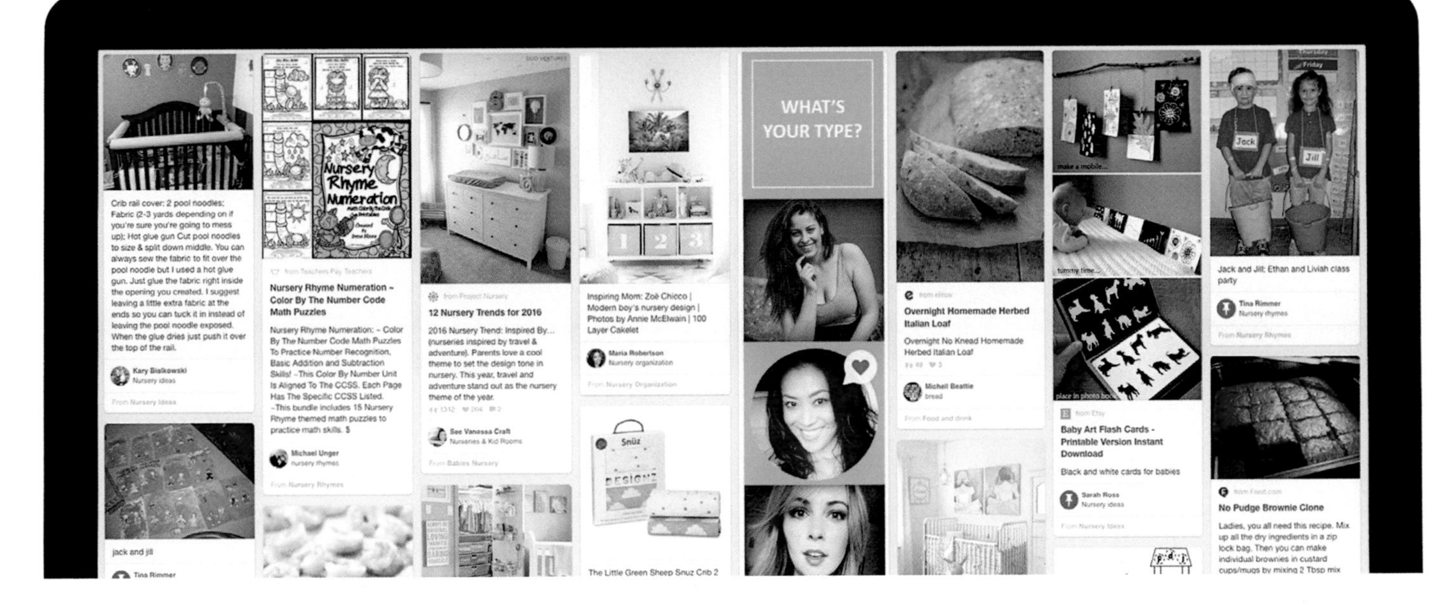

ACTUAL CLIENT STORY:
GIDGET & JOHN

WE USED FACEBOOK *to announce we were beginning the adoption process. We posted this in April and adopted our son in October of the same year. My sister halfway across the country read my post and three days later was in a bar where she overheard a woman talking about her pregnant daughter who was looking for an adoptive family.*

My sister butted into the conversation and within 24 hours I was connected through email with the most amazing birth mother. She chose life, my husband and I as parents and she changed our lives forever. I will never stop praying for her and the birth father.

My sister kind of knew we were considering adoption but it wasn't until she saw my Facebook post that she was on high alert.

HOME FEED

When you sign into your account, you will see a home feed, much like Facebook's news feed. These are all topics, articles and ideas that relate to the interests you shared when you set up your account. You can adjust those settings at any time in your profile settings. Scroll through your home feed for fresh ideas!

GAINING FOLLOWERS

Since you are on a mission to expand your adoption outreach, let's talk a bit about how to gain more followers. Here are a few ideas on how to grow your audience:

- Share often on your Pinterest page. Try to post every few days and not all at once. This will allow your pins to show up in others' feeds at different times.
- Share original content, which includes your own images, quotes, or photos. Original content will always link back to your boards or Pinterest page and gain more attention.
- Share other pins that you love. Make sure to add your keywords or keyword phrases and a link back to your website or a social media page in original posts and others' pins.

YOUTUBE

How to set up an account on Youtube.

DID YOU KNOW? ***YouTube is too often ignored by those who don't understand its scope or reach. In an average month, 8 out of 10 18-49 year-olds watch YouTube. YouTube is the world's second largest search engine and third most visited site after Google and Facebook. Let me repeat that... YouTube is the world's second largest search engine and third most visited site after Google and Facebook. The power of YouTube is that it's a resource for learning just about anything plus a highly-engaging entertainment platform. It's "sticky" and users spend more time per-session on YouTube than on Facebook or Instagram combined.***

1. CREATE A NEW ACCOUNT by filling out the neccesary information and agreeing to the Terms and Privacy.
2. USE AN EXISTING GMAIL ACCOUNT by clicking on the app launcher in the top right corner of your gmail and selecting YouTube.

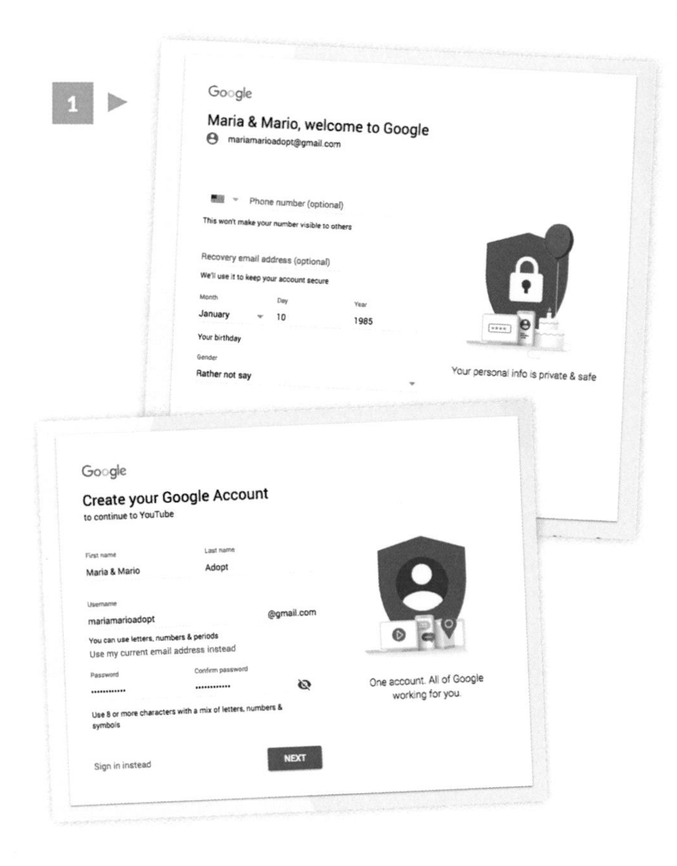

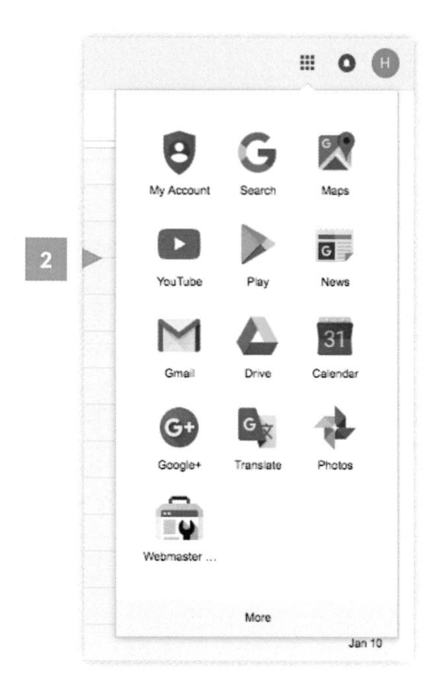

OTHER MEDIA PLATFORMS REQUIRE ON-GOING INVESTMENT OF YOUR TIME AND ENERGY, YOUTUBE ONLY REQUIRES PRODUCING AND UPLOADING A VIDEO.

3. FINISH YOUR ACCOUNT by clicking on the circle icon next to your gmail name. A dropdown list will appear, select "creator studio".

4. CREATE A CHANNEL In Creator Studio, a page will appear that says "You must create a channel to upload videos. Create a channel." Click "Create a channel".

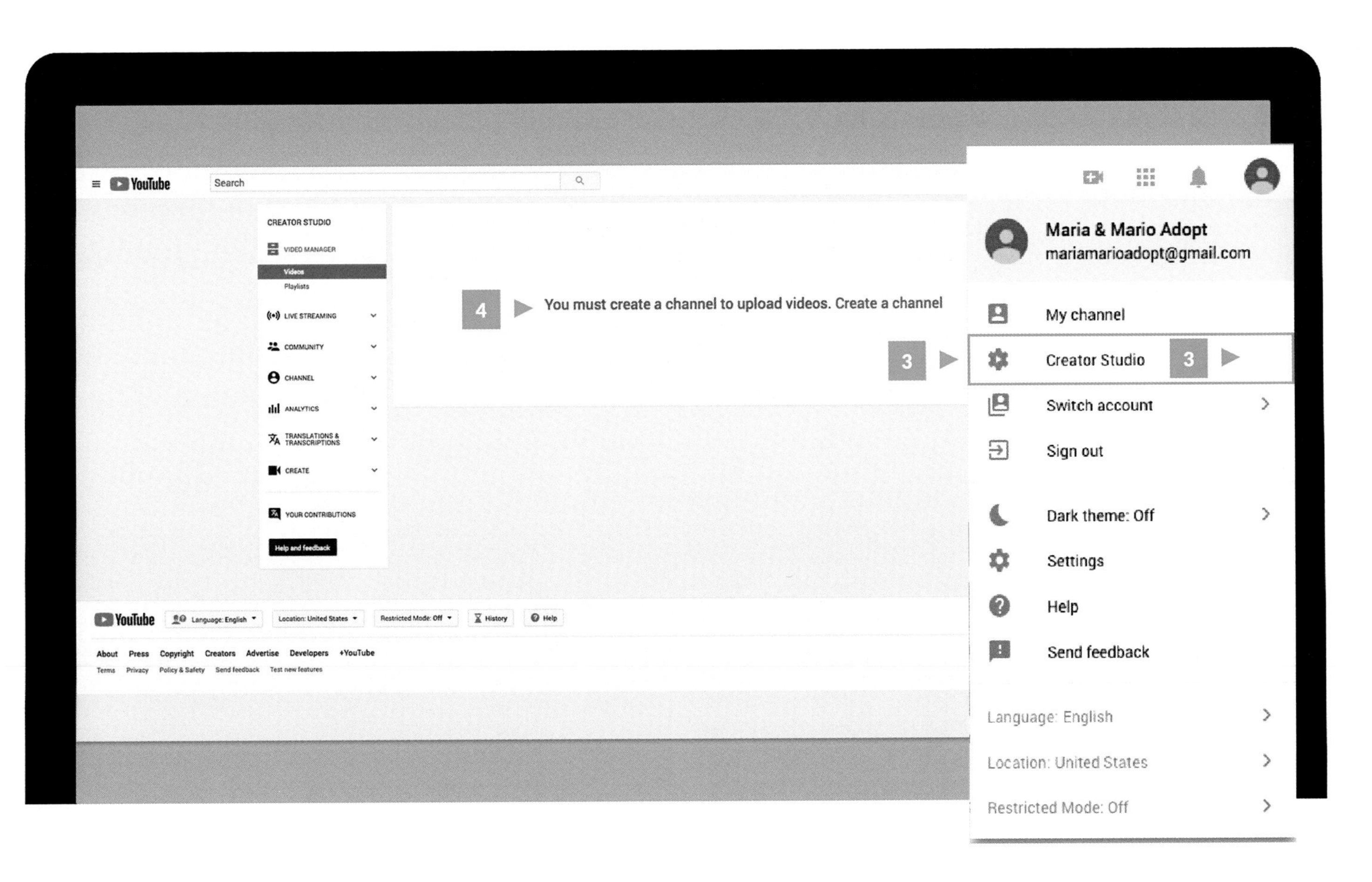

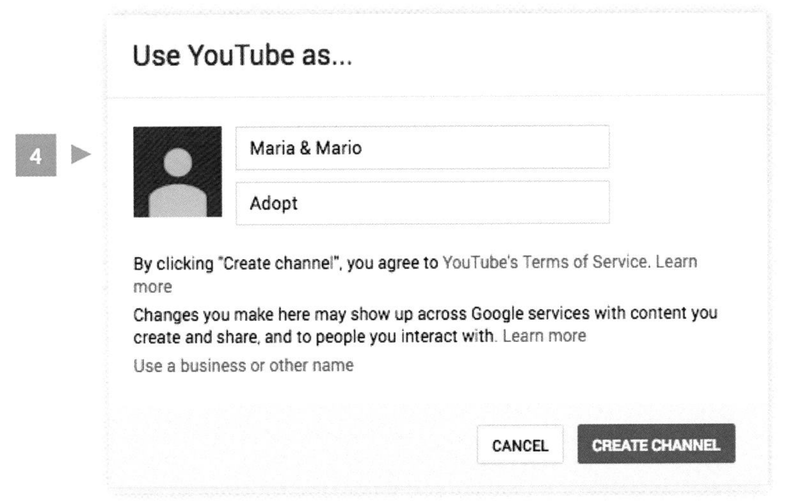

4. NAME YOUR CHANNEL you can change your name later, but be cautious YouTube limits the number of times you can change the name of your channel.

YOUTUBE IS OWNED BY GOOGLE! SINCE YOUTUBE IS WHOLLY OWNED BY GOOGLE IT SHOULD BE NO SURPRISE VIDEOS ON YOUTUBE RANK HIGHLY IN SEARCH RESULTS.

YOUTUBE

Customizing your channel

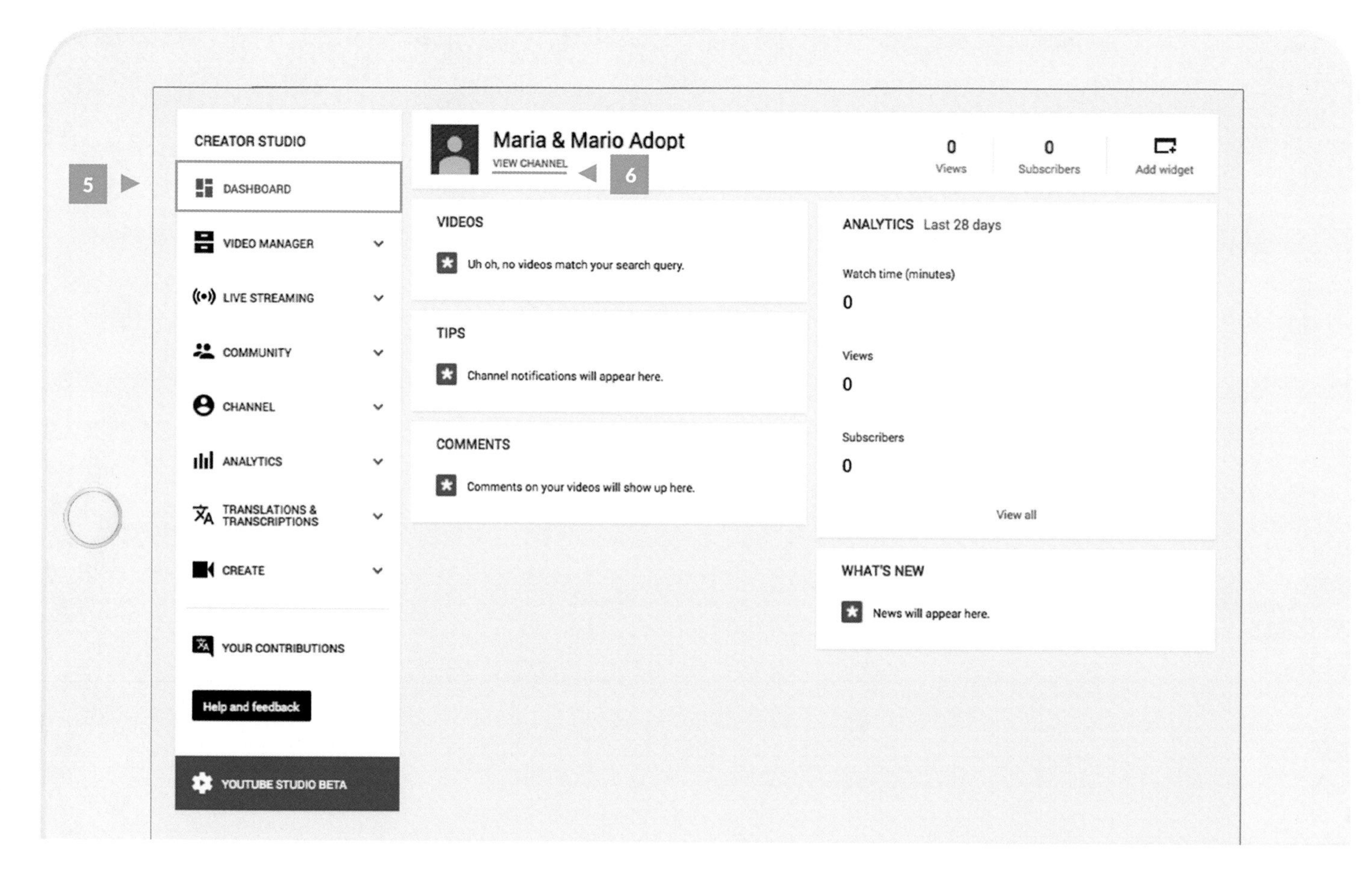

5. DASHBOARD select "Dashboard" on the left menu bar for an overview of your channel. This is where all of the important information regarding your channel will appear. Your videos, Tips, Comments, Analytics and what's new.

6. VIEW CHANNEL to see what your channel looks like and to customization options.

7. CUSTOMIZE your channel by uploading a picture and channel art. Your channel art should be 1250px by 1440px and no larger than 6MB.

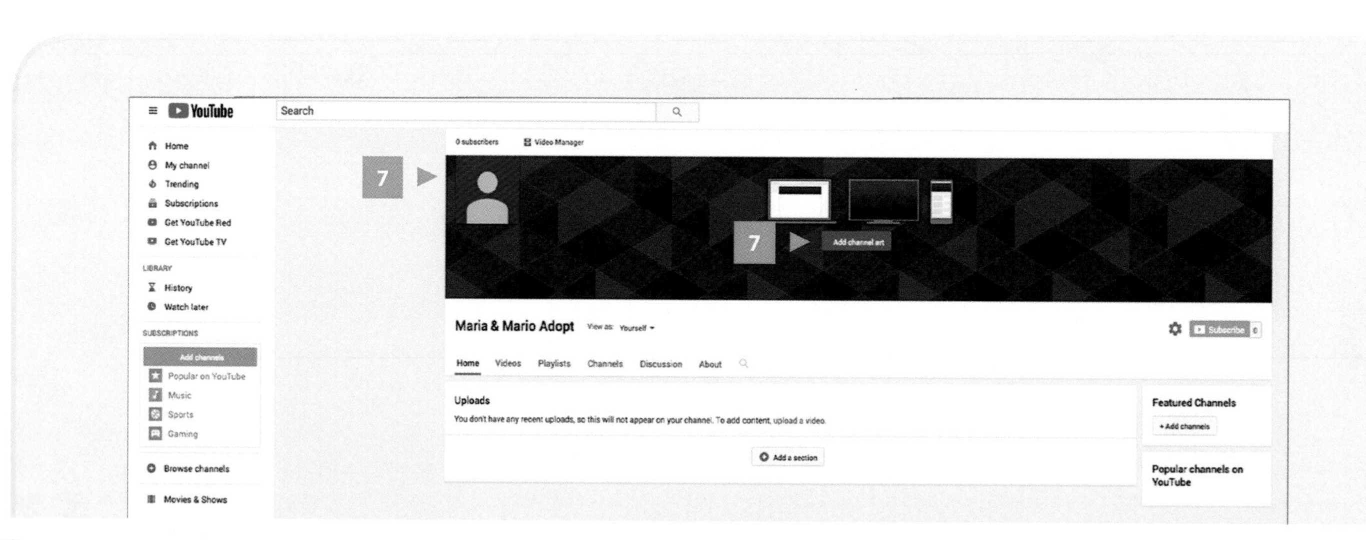

NOW THAT YOUR ACCOUNT IS SET UP IT'S TIME TO UPLOAD YOUR CONTENT! *You decide what kind of user you'd like to be on YouTube:*

- *Entry Level: Create a Brand Account and Channel, paying particular attention to fields for keywords. Write rich, keyword embedded copy describing any videos you upload to make them searchable. Produce and upload 3-5 "how to" videos.*
- *Moderate but Committed: Link your channel to your other media accounts, and promote your videos cross-platform.*
- *Master Level: Create an on-going series, or a linked set of videos to encourage serial viewing.*

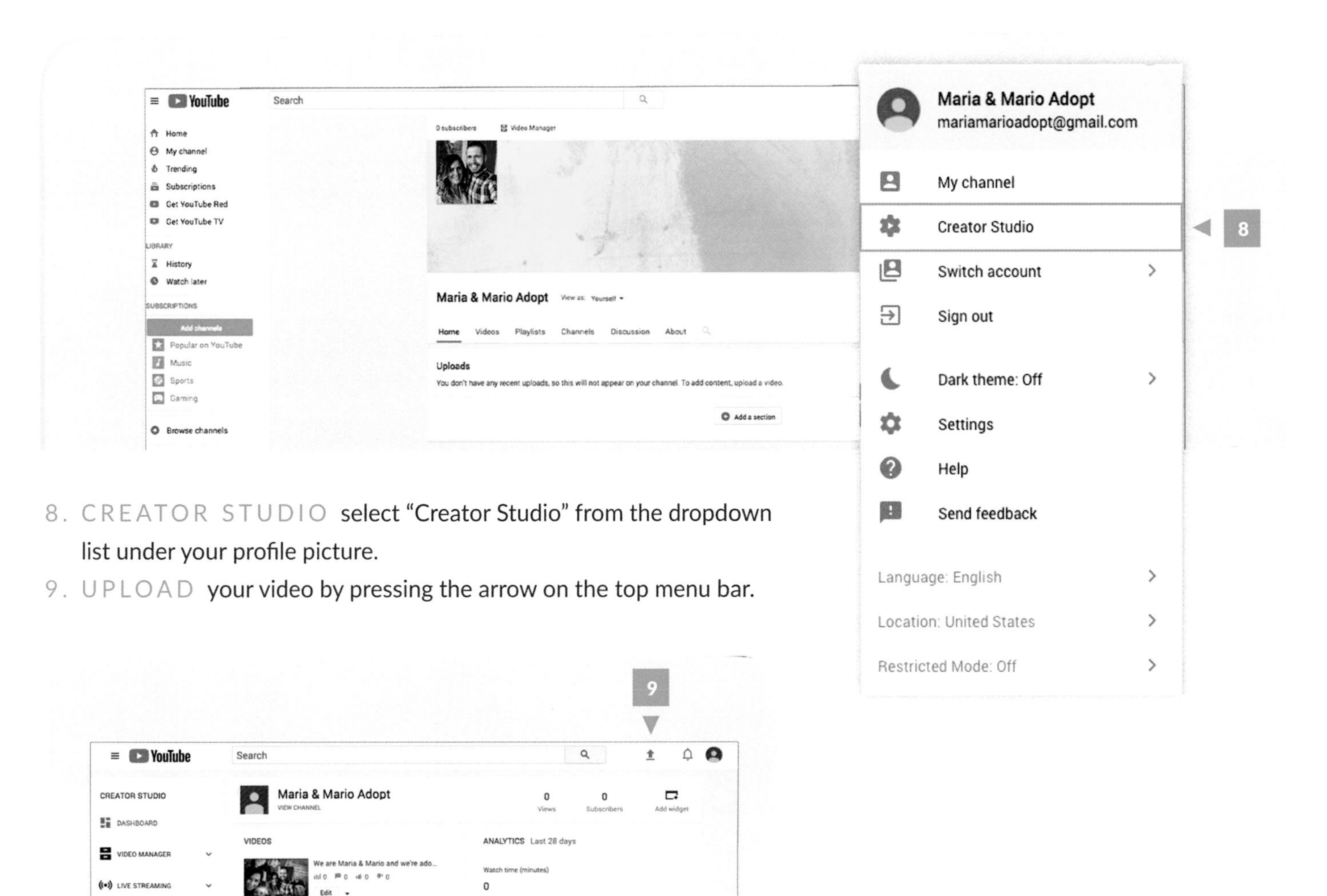

8. CREATOR STUDIO select "Creator Studio" from the dropdown list under your profile picture.
9. UPLOAD your video by pressing the arrow on the top menu bar.

10. NAME your video something relevant and searchable - be as specific as possible!
11. DESCRIPTION is important! The more detailed and more keywords that you use, the better. You can also link other social media accounts here.
12. TAGS and keywords are key to your video's visibility. Use as many descriptive words that are relevant to your video.

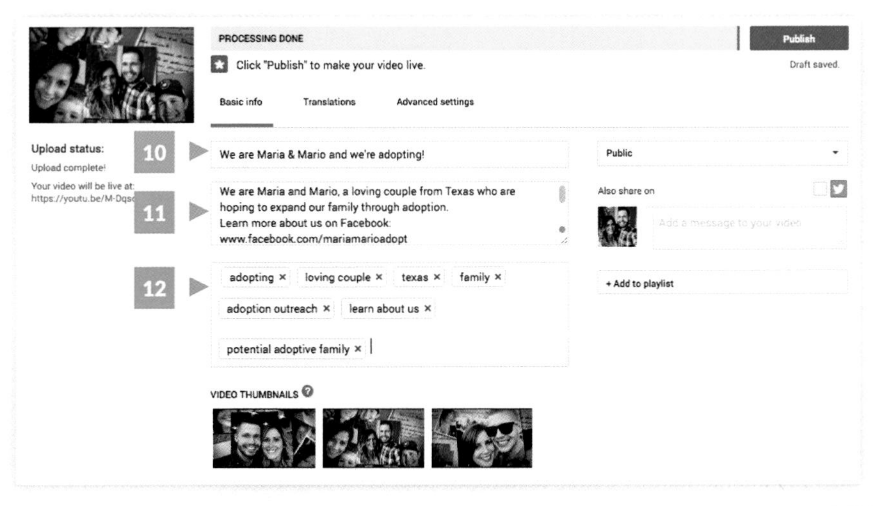

NOTES:

YOU'VE ADDED
FIVE PIECES!

1 CREATE FACEBOOK PAGE 2 INSTAGRAM 3 PINTEREST  4 TWITTER 5 LINK EVERYTHING

NEXT STEPS

TOPICS COVERED IN THIS SECTION:

- Creating a Marketing Campaign
- Setting Attainable Goals
- Best Times to Post Content Online
- Account Names & Passwords

MARKETING CAMPAIGN

How to bring everything together.

IF YOU HAVE MADE IT THIS FAR, ***congratulations! We've shared a lot of content and you might be feeling a bit overwhelmed. Let's take a minute to enjoy a deep breath. Better? Great, now that you are feeling more relaxed, let's start making a plan on how to pull all this information together for your adoption outreach.***

CHOOSE YOUR ONLINE PLATFORM

Although the impulse may be to begin your outreach by engaging on each and every social media platform, we recommend starting more slowly and mastering each platform before layering on another. Paying attention to the details really makes an enormous difference, so dig deep into each platform rather then skim the surface on all of them.

MAKE SOME GOALS

Create some goals and approach them as if they were tasks at work. It's easy to run headlong into the world of social media, and it's easy to get lost when you don't have a plan of action.

Examples of goals:

- On Facebook, comment on 10 posts from other people that relate to my adoption journey.

- On Instagram, find 10-20 adoption-related accounts and "follow" them. These can be other hopeful adoptive parents, adoption agencies, adoption service providers, etc.

- Publish three new blog posts per week for one month.

- Hang up one pull-tab flyer at a new location every week for two months.

- For more examples of goals, see the next page!

EVALUATE

After you arrive at an initial goal date, examine how your goals worked. Were they successful? Would another approach work better? Are my goals too large to accomplish with my other activities in life? Do I feel comfortable with the steps I've taken so far and can I now expand my outreach?

INVEST IN WHAT IS WORKING

Once you have dipped your toes in the water and have met some goals, look at what is working for you and what might not be a good use of your time. You might be posting regularly on your blog but are you seeing any real feedback? Are you generating any new interest? You might be spending money on Facebook ads but are they accomplishing anything? Do you see results that are making it worth the investment? Don't forget to take a little time every so often and look at what is generating interest and providing fruitful outreach and what is more work than it's worth.

NOTE: *Don't give up on anything too quickly (especially if it is free) but make sure to keep an eye on your overall goals. Keep in mind that in the beginning most of your efforts will go towards widening your net by gaining "likes" and followers.*

SET UP ACCOUNTS FOR ALL THE SOCIAL MEDIA PLATFORMS YOU WANT AND LINK THEM TOGETHER. MASTER THEM ONE AT A TIME BEFORE YOU MOVE ONTO THE NEXT!

GOALS TO CONSIDER FOR GENERAL OUTREACH:

- Try to give out at least two outreach cards every week for the next three months.
- Email networking letters to 20 contacts and, if you don't hear anything, follow-up with all of them in six weeks to remind them of your hope to adopt.
- Ask 5-10 friends to be a part of your social media "team" for a specific amount of time (one month, three months, etc.). They will "like" and post responses on your content as well as share your content on their social media accounts. After the time period is over, get feedback from your team on what types of content are getting the most response and attention.
- Learn to schedule posts in advance so you can ensure you're posting at peak times regardless of where you are or what you're doing at the time.
- Reach out to 1-2 adoption blogs and follow them. Ask if they will follow your blog and cross-post one another's content.
- Share 2-3 of your favorite blog posts and stories on your social media page, website or blog.
- Check out the Hopefully Parents blog every week for new ideas and inspiration!

GOALS TO CONSIDER FOR FACEBOOK:

- Before you begin outreach, populate your Facebook community page with photos of activities you enjoy and think about how each photo relates to the brand you are creating. Within one week, create 20 posts so the page is populated and active when you invite your family and friends to "like" your page.
- Get 100 people to "like" or "follow" your adoption outreach Facebook page.
- Post something new on your page three times a week for one month. Try sharing a video as well as pictures!
- Think about something interesting to share and go "live" on Facebook. Share a live video twice a month.
- Try to post something that generates at least 50 "likes" and/or 10 comments from viewers.

GOALS TO CONSIDER FOR INSTAGRAM:

- Add 10-15 photos to your account and then invite friends and family to follow you. Get over 50 followers in your first month.
- Pick 2-3 hashtags (keywords) and make sure to include those on every photo. Once you have that down, research new hashtags that are commonly used and could go well with your adoption journey, then add those to your photos too.
- Use Instagram Stories once a week for one month.
- Find 5-10 new groups or users to follow each week that relate to your adoption journey.

PEAK TIMES

Best times to post content online.

CREATING MEANINGFUL CONTENT *that resonates with your friends and fans is a great first step, and the next step is to post that content at peak times so more people see and interact with your posts. Different platforms have different audiences and this can affect everything from how long they spend on the platform to the time they're most active. My Clever Agency (mycleveragency.com) has gathered the optimum times for each social site so you can make the hard work you put into your content worth it.*

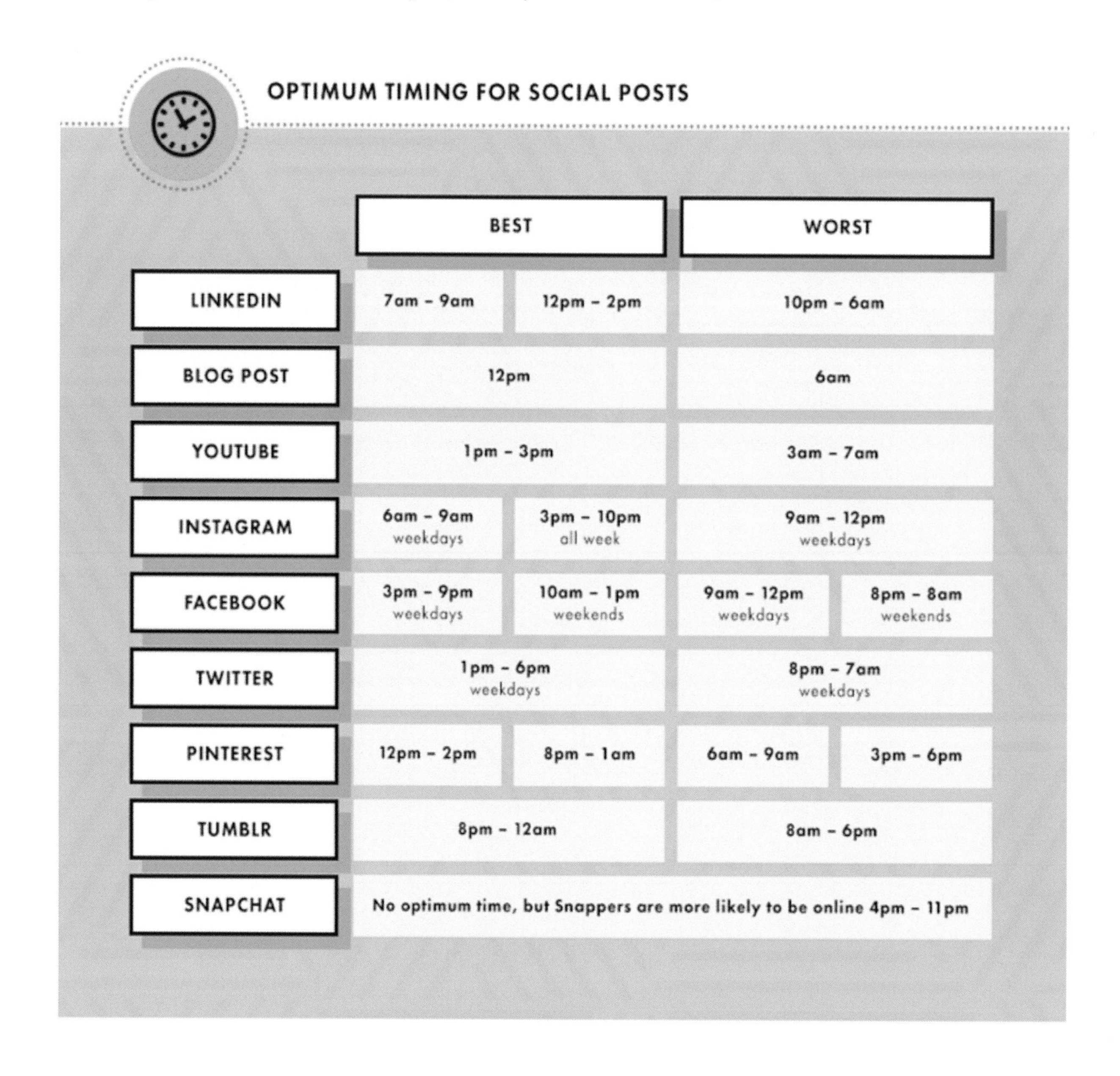

OPTIMUM TIMING FOR SOCIAL POSTS

	BEST		WORST	
LINKEDIN	7am - 9am	12pm - 2pm	10pm - 6am	
BLOG POST	12pm		6am	
YOUTUBE	1pm - 3pm		3am - 7am	
INSTAGRAM	6am - 9am weekdays	3pm - 10pm all week	9am - 12pm weekdays	
FACEBOOK	3pm - 9pm weekdays	10am - 1pm weekends	9am - 12pm weekdays	8pm - 8am weekends
TWITTER	1pm - 6pm weekdays		8pm - 7am weekdays	
PINTEREST	12pm - 2pm	8pm - 1am	6am - 9am	3pm - 6pm
TUMBLR	8pm - 12am		8am - 6pm	
SNAPCHAT	No optimum time, but Snappers are more likely to be online 4pm - 11pm			

SOURCE

THE CHART ABOVE IS FROM 'MY CLEVER AGENCY' IN THEIR SOCIAL MEDIA WHITE PAPER.

mycleveragency.com/whitepapers/how-to-create-perfect-posts-on-social-platforms

ACCOUNTS

Names and passwords.

IT CAN BE DIFFICULT TO REMEMBER *all of the different account names and passwords you use when setting up social media accounts, blogs, etc. Here is a place to write everything down, keep track of it and keep it secure!*

WEBSITE	USER NAME/LOGIN	PASSWORD

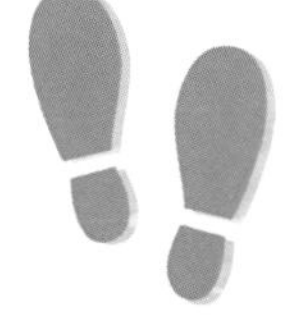

ACTUAL CLIENT STORY:
SHANNON & JONATHAN

SOCIAL MEDIA IS WHAT LED US TO OUR SON. *As part of our adoption outreach, we started a blog to document our journey. Our agency offered to host one of our posts about patience on their site. I wrote it from the perspective of having patience while waiting to be matched. Our birth mom (who was searching our agency's site for prospective parents) read it and it completely resonated with her. She immediately went to our blog and called us that afternoon.*

We matched a month later and now have a beautiful one-year-old son. Social media is such a powerful tool, you never know how far it will reach. Its platform is so vast and it can link you to people in a way nothing else can. We know without a doubt that it helped give us the family we always dreamed of.

NOTES:

YOU'VE ADDED
THREE PIECES!

1 CREATING A MARKETING PLAN 2 MAKE GOALS 3 MASTER PEAK TIMES

FIRST CONTACT

TOPICS COVERED IN THIS SECTION:

- Preparing for Your First Contact with an Expectant Family
- Joanna's Story—Don't Give Up!
- Social Media Scams
- Being Aware of Red Flags

FIRST CONTACT

Preparing for contact with expectant families.

AT SOME POINT ***you are going to be contacted by someone that wants to talk seriously about adoption and a possible placement. When you are beginning your journey it may feel like that day will never come, but it will, and it's helpful to think about how you will handle that first call or text. Let's take a few moments to think about and prepare for that initial contact. Here are some useful hints to help you along!***

Keep the first conversation easy and light and let her direct the questions. Feel free to answer her questions and reply with similar questions back. For instance, if she asks how old you are, answer, and then you may ask, "How old are you?" This keeps the conversation flowing and lets her control the subject matter and depth of the conversation.

THINGS TO ASK:

- Ask about the expectant father, if he is involved and supportive, or some general questions about him.
- Ask who is providing emotional support to her during this difficult time.
- Ask why she is considering adoption.
- Ask if she is considering adoption in general or if she is actively looking for families.
- Ask what her plans are after the baby is born.
- Ask about her parents, family or friends and if they are supportive of her plans to place her baby for adoption.

THINGS TO AVOID:

- Any questions regarding drug or alcohol use.
- If she thinks she will change her mind.
- Demanding proof of pregnancy before you have a chance to get to know one another.
- If she will she need living expenses.

NOTE: *Your agency or attorney should handle all delicate questions like those above. You focus on getting to know one another and let them ask the hard questions.*

PROFESSIONAL ADVICE
ADOPTIONS OF WISCONSIN

As quickly as possible, you should ensure the expectant parents are referred to your agency so they can offer the appropriate support and counseling. They may request proof of pregnancy and discuss financial support, if necessary. These are tricky areas, so let your adoption professional handle them!

NOTE: Your attorney or agency will advise you on the specifics regarding "expectant parent expenses" that are allowed in your state. Do not send money or gifts without consulting them first!

HELPFUL HINT

MOST FIRST CONTACT COMES VIA TEXTING!

IT'S NOT ALL ROSES

Scams and cautions on social media.

SOCIAL MEDIA *is a great tool to use in order to connect with family, friends and to meet new people. Sadly, there is also a dark side to social media because it also allows people to use these applications when they don't have the best intentions. The more educated you are about adoption scams, the more confident you will feel when meeting and interacting with expectant parents. Here are a few tips to help recognize and avoid scammers:*

- If someone is resistant to getting in contact with your adoption case worker or attorney, be careful. They might just be shy or hesitant, but their hesitation might also be a red flag that they either aren't serious about adoption or that they don't want to be found out if they have less than honorable intentions.

- Sonogram photos are quite easy to fake. It takes about five minutes to buy a fake sonogram photo online, complete with any name, date and hospital name printed on it. A sonogram photo should never be accepted as proof of pregnancy.

- Other photos are easy to pirate as well. Make sure to do a "reverse image search" on Google or TinEye to see if the photo is being used elsewhere on the web.

- If someone contacts you and it seems a little fishy, search for this person on various social media platforms. It is typical for someone to have accounts on other platforms if they are an actual person. If you do not find social media accounts with the name of the person you are communicating with, it can be a red flag.

- You can join the "Adoption Scams" group on Facebook and look for other "Adoption Scams" pages or groups on social media to stay on top of current scams and potential scammers.

- Not all scams involve financial gain. Scammers will sometimes seek your time, attention and emotional connection. Watch out for emotional leeches!

IT'S VERY POSSIBLE THAT YOU WILL BE IN CONTACT WITH SEVERAL EXPECTANT PARENTS AT THE SAME TIME.

KEEP A NOTEBOOK WITH A LOG OF ALL CONVERSATIONS SO YOU CAN REFER BACK TO YOUR NOTES WHEN YOU'RE COMMUNICATING WITH SOMEONE.

THIS WILL HELP CATCH A SCAMMER SINCE THEY ARE OFTEN MAKING UP LIES ON THE SPOT AND WON'T BE AS GOOD AT KEEPING THINGS STRAIGHT.

IT'S NOT ALL ROSES

Red flags when talking with an expectant family.

ONCE YOU HAVE CONNECTED *with an expectant family, you will want to listen closely for little clues that could signal a red flag or something that doesn't quite add up. In the excitement of making connections and feeling like your dreams of becoming a parent are closer to coming true, you will want to take a few deep breaths and make sure you aren't wasting your time and talking with someone who doesn't have your best interests at heart. Below are some possible red flags to watch out for:*

- She makes a plan to let you parent the baby but then still needs to "get to know you better."
- She makes plans to meet or speak on the phone but never follows through or always has an excuse.
- She overshares personal information, placing you in a position of acting out of guilt or sympathy.
- She is in a rush to place her already-born baby right away and wants to skip counseling offered by your agency.
- She doesn't provide factual evidence or medical records of a pregnancy to your attorney or adoption professional.
- She texts you often and at inappropriate times and gets upset when you don't reply or engage right away.
- She wants to make a plan to bring the baby to you, rather than meet at a hospital or your agency or attorney's office. This includes you purchasing airline tickets for her that can then be cashed in later.
- She forgets details you have shared with her—a sign she might be talking to multiple families at the same time.
- She constantly needs financial help or compensation in some way.
- You connect with someone who "knows" about a pregnant relative or friend but you are not able to connect with her personally.
- It seems like she has one or more crises going on and her answer to the problem involves you. Be sensitive but cautious.
- She is always the one who calls you and won't provide a phone number or any way to contact her directly.
- She says you are perfect and is trying to match very quickly without really getting to know you or arranging to meet.

PROFESSIONAL ADVICE
MY ADOPTION ADVISOR

In addition to strengthening your awareness of scams, we also suggest you determine your risk tolerance. Consider how much time and money you're willing to invest in someone before they provide REAL proof of pregnancy and meet with an attorney or social worker face-to-face.

When speaking with adopting parents who have been victimized, most admit that deep down they felt like something wasn't right, but they didn't want to believe it. Listen to your inner voice and trust your instincts!

To learn more about this topic, check out our eLearning course, Identify Red Flags & Avoid Adoption Scams. Sometimes it's good to learn through experience. This is NOT one of those times! http://www.myadoptionadvisor.com/services/adoption-training

- She is very reluctant to talk to anyone else about her pregnancy or adoption plans such as an attorney or adoption social worker and only wants to talk to you.

- Pictures, proof of pregnancy, medical records and other documents such as these that she agrees to share with you never arrive.

- She wants money or financial assistance of some type without going through proper channels. Money should never be given directly to an expectant mother - doing so could be viewed as coercion and could cause your placement to be denied in court. Payments and assistance should always be conducted through a qualified adoption professional that is familiar with federal and state laws regarding this type of help.

- If something seems off to you, trust your gut! Most times in a scam, the warning signs are there, you just need to be willing to see them.

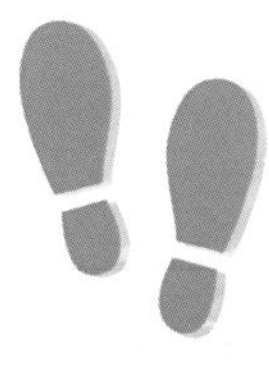

ACTUAL CLIENT STORY:
SARAH & JOHN

▲ Shortly after submitting this story, Sarah and John matched and adopted a son, pictured here!

IF I AM BEING TOTALLY HONEST WITH YOU, *most of our social networking has only brought us emotional scammers. People pretending to be pregnant and leading us on, only to be exposed later as toying with us.*

Other than that, I guess we have had many people following us and it's never bad to have more people aware of our adoption wait. I used to blog/Facebook/tweet/Instagram often, but coming up on the 2.5 years of waiting mark and another birthday around the corner, I'm not feeling very into it.

I think that social media is great if the right person sees it at the right time. We haven't been lucky enough for that to happen yet. I think social media networking for adoption also takes a lot of getting used to. It can be really exhausting to keep up all of the accounts.

Many people network constantly (including us for the last couple of years) and wait a very long time, and many people never network and adopt quickly. There isn't really any rhyme or reason to it.

Social networking for adoption makes you feel like you are doing something to help it happen, but I am convinced it will happen when it happens no matter what you do.

JOANNA'S STORY

Don't give up: A story of heartbreak and hope.

Just like life, adoption does not always happen in the way we expect it to or in the way we want it to, but trust that it will happen in exactly the way it should.

My name is Joanna, and I am an adult adoptee as well as an adoptive mama. I work in the field of adoption as the owner of Our Chosen Child Adoption Profile Design Service and Hopefully Parents. I have been an advocate for adoption my entire life. I believe deeply that adoption is a spiritual contract that brings families together with an unbreakable bond—the love of a child.

Many years ago my husband and I embarked on our own adoption journey much like you are now. We had a 2 ½ year old son, our miracle baby, and we knew we wanted more children. Our son was our fourth in vitro attempt, and his twin brother passed away at birth so we knew we could not walk that road again. Because I was adopted it was always my intention to adopt a child, and so began our adoption journey.

We started working with a local agency, and although they were great, I quickly grew restless with "the wait." Patience is a virtue, but it wasn't one of MY virtues so I began to search online for other outreach methods to help us adopt. I quickly plugged into every adoption-related website available and began posting our profile and submitting our documents to situations that were posted online. A few months later we were contacted by a young expectant mom who wanted to talk to us. After many conversations she shared that she knew we were the right family for her baby.

Jo, the expectant mom, was living in a maternity home at the time (yes, they existed even a few years ago!) and was very unhappy there. We agreed to pay to move her closer to home on the condition that she tell her mother she was pregnant and considering adoption. Not only did we want her to have the support of family, but we wanted the adoption to be completely above-board and ethical. As the months went on we formed an amazing relationship with Jo and her mother. We even got to the point of sharing holiday recipes so this baby would know both of our families' traditions. We were ecstatic.

Finally, we got "the call." We raced to the airport and flew down to join Jo at the hospital and meet our new son. Watching our older son holding this new baby was unlike anything I had ever felt—love on top of love on top of love. But from the highest high we quickly fell to the lowest of the low. Three days later Jo changed her mind, and we felt the earth crumble under our feet. We returned home, and I left the suitcase full of baby clothes and diapers by the front door, went to bed and thought I would never get up again.

◄ *Best friends from the beginning, Mac and Marcus*

But then the universe, in all her wisdom, intervened. A social worker I had met earlier in our journey reached out about a baby boy that was alone in a hospital on the other side of the country. She asked if we wanted to submit our profile. Without telling my husband I said yes, and then stood in the shower and let the tears rain down until I didn't have anything left. We were completely broken, and I held onto this one small ray of hope like it was my lifeline.

Three days later at seven o'clock at night the phone rang, and we learned we were parents again. Before dawn the next morning I walked to the front door, picked up the suitcase I had left there a week ago, and boarded a plane to meet our new son.

Let me tell you about our son. There isn't a single day I am not grateful for the crooked road that brought him to us. He is worth every tear, every heartbreak, and every dark, dark night in our year-long adoption journey. We have two miracle children, and our hearts are full and our family complete. I could have never imagined in a million years the path we had to walk when we started trying to have a family and make our dreams come true. Would I do it again? A million times and more if it meant we would have the family we do today.

DON'T GIVE UP! The road may be long, and it may be crooked, and it may take more than you thought you had in you, but don't give up. Your future is waiting for you, and you need to be there to meet it.

▲ *Joanna and her whole happy family today! Pictured left to right, Mac, Jack, Joanna and Marcus*

NOTES:

YOU'VE ADDED
THREE PIECES!

1 PREPARE FOR CONTACT 2 SELF-CARE 3 CHECK FOR SCAMS

ADVERTISING LAWS BY STATE

TOPICS COVERED IN THIS SECTION:

- Information on Every State Regarding Adoption Advertising Laws
- Specific Citations on Record
- “Bottom Line” Information on Legal Status of Advertising in Each State

LAWS BY STATE

Some guidelines on advertising in your state.

DISCLAIMER: ***Hopefully Parents encourages (and recommends) checking with an adoption attorney in your state or adoption agency before advertising in your state or beyond. Hopefully Parents is neither responsible for, or authorized to give legal advice relating to adoption advertising. Always use caution when advertising and make sure to read up on scams, red flags and cautions before getting started.*** LAWS CURRENT AS OF 2015, PLEASE CHECK WITH YOUR ATTORNEY FOR RECENT UPDATES.

The following list of adoption advertising laws per state can be your starting point when it comes to understanding what you legally can and cannot do to advertise your desire to adopt. Presenting you with this information should not be considered legal advice nor should it be relied upon as you make decisions. This information is your guide in starting to understand what may or may not be allowed. You should also meet with a qualified adoption attorney to discuss more specifics and make final decisions.

The "Bottom Line" stated in teal at the beginning of each section focuses on whether prospective adoptive parents can place adoption ads. It is not meant to comment on what attorneys or agencies are legally allowed to do, as these might differ.

Please also keep in mind that just because you are a resident of a state that prohibits advertising, that doesn't necessarily mean you cannot advertise in a state that allows it. Similarly, just because you reside in a state that allows advertising, it doesn't mean you can advertise in other states that prohibit it. Discuss these and other specific topics with your experienced adoption attorney.

ALABAMA

Bottom Line: Advertising is Prohibited

Citation: Ala. Code § 26-10A-36

It shall be unlawfwul for any person, organization, corporation, partnership, hospital, association, or agency to advertise verbally, through print, electronic media, or otherwise that they will adopt children or assist in the adoption of children.

ALASKA

Bottom Line: Advertising is Allowed

This issue is not addressed in the statutes reviewed.

ARIZONA

Bottom Line: Advertising is Allowed

This issue is not addressed in the statutes reviewed.

ARKANSAS

Bottom Line: Advertising is Allowed

This issue is not addressed in the statutes reviewed.

CALIFORNIA

Bottom Line: Advertising is Prohibited

Citation: Family Law § 8609(a)

No person or organization may advertise in any periodical or newspaper or by radio or other public medium that he, she, or it will place or provide children for adoption, or cause any advertisement to be published in any public medium soliciting, requesting, or asking for any child or children for adoption, unless that person or organization is licensed to place children for adoption by the department.

SOURCE

THE INFORMATION ON PAGES 118-127 IS FROM THE CHILD WELFARE INFORMATION GATEWAY.

- It is not legal to use Facebook advertising.

- It is not legal to use Google Ads. California must be blocked if you set up ads in Google.

- It is legal to use Facebook to share your journey, as long as you do not state that you are looking for an expectant parent. Sharing a community page is perfectly fine.

COLORADO

Bottom Line: Advertising is Allowed

Citation: Rev. Stat. § 19-5-213.5

The term 'advertise through a public medium' means to communicate by any public medium such as a newspaper, periodical, telephone book listing, outdoor advertising sign, radio, television, or computerized communication system, including an Internet site, an Internet profile,
or any similar medium of communication provided via the Internet.

This section does not apply to an individual who has received a favorable home study recommendation regarding his or her fitness to be an adoptive parent.

CONNECTICUT

Bottom Line: Advertising is Allowed

Citation: Ann. Stat. § 45a-728d

Any prospective adoptive parent may advertise through any public media in this State for placement of a child into his or her care for the purpose of adoption.

DELAWARE

Bottom Line: Advertising is Prohibited

Citation: Ann. Code Tit. 13, § 930

Only the Department of Services for Children, Youth and their Families or a licensed agency may advertise in this State regarding the availability of adoption services or for the placement of a child for the purpose of adoption.

DISTRICT OF COLUMBIA

Bottom Line: Advertising is Allowed

This issue is not addressed in the statutes reviewed.

FLORIDA

Bottom Line: Advertising is Prohibited

Citation: Ann. Stat. § 63.212(1)(g)

It is unlawful for any person, except an adoption entity, to advertise or offer to the public, in any way, by any medium whatever, that a minor is available for adoption or that a minor is sought for adoption; it is unlawful for any person to publish or broadcast any such advertisement without including the Florida license number of the agency or attorney placing the advertisement.

The term 'adoption entity' includes the Department of Children and Families, a registered child-caring agency, an intermediary, a Florida licensed child-placing agency, or a child-placing agency licensed in another State that also is licensed by the department to place children in the State of Florida.

GEORGIA

Bottom Line: Advertising is Prohibited

Citation: Ann. Code § 19-8-24(a)(!), (d)

It shall be unlawful for any person, organization, corporation, hospital, or association that has not been established as a child-placing agency by the department to advertise, whether in a periodical, by television, radio, or any other public medium or private means, that the person, organization, corporation, hospital, or association will adopt children or will arrange for children to be placed for adoption. Individuals seeking to adopt a child or to place their child for adoption may communicate by private means, which include only written letters or oral statements.

- It is legal to use letters to network, as long as they don't mention using an attorney.

- It is legal to share your interest in adopting as long as it is in a non-promotional way.

- It is not legal to advertise any financial assistance or exchange of monetary offerings like medical bills, counseling, housing, etc.

- It is not legal to use public media to advertise such as television, radio, newspapers, etc.

HAWAII

Bottom Line: Advertising is Allowed

This issue is not addressed in the statutes reviewed.

IDAHO

Bottom Line: Advertising is Prohibited

Citation: Ann. Code § 18-1512A

No person or entity shall publish or broadcast on radio or television an advertisement or notice of a child or children offered or wanted for adoption, or claim through such advertisement to have the ability to place, locate, dispose, or receive a child or children for adoption, unless the person or entity is a duly authorized agent or employee of the Department of Health and Welfare or an institution licensed by the department to care for and place children.

This section is not intended to prohibit:

- A licensed attorney from advertising his or her ability to practice or provide services related to the adoption of children.

- Physicians and other health-care providers from assisting or providing natural and adoptive parents with medical care necessary to initiate and complete adoptive placements.

ILLINOIS

Bottom Line: Advertising is Allowed

Citation: Cons. Stat. Tit. 225, § 10/12

A person, group of persons, agency, association, organization, corporation, institution, center, or group that advertises or publishes any advertisement offering, soliciting, or promising to perform adoption services is guilty of a misdemeanor and shall be subject to a fine, unless they are:

- Licensed or operating under a permit issued by the department as a child care facility or child welfare agency.

- An expectant parent or a prospective adoptive parent acting on his or her own behalf.

- A licensed attorney advertising his or her availability to provide legal services relating to adoption, as permitted by law.

INDIANA

Bottom Line: Advertising is Prohibited

Citation: Ann. Code § 35-46-1-21

Only a licensed attorney or a licensed child-placing agency may place a paid advertisement or paid listing of a person's telephone number, on that person's own behalf, in a telephone directory that a child is offered or wanted for adoption, or that person is able to place, locate, or receive a child for adoption.

IOWA

Bottom Line: Advertising is Allowed

This issue is not addressed in the statutes reviewed.

KANSAS

Bottom Line: Advertising is Allowed

Citation: Ann. Stat. § 59-2123(a)(1), (b)-(c)

Any person who advertises that such person will adopt, find an adoptive home for a child, or otherwise place a child for adoption shall state in such advertisement whether or not such person is licensed and if licensed, under what authority such license is issued and in what profession.

This provision shall not apply to the Kansas Department for Children and Families or to an individual seeking to adopt a child.

The term 'advertise' means to communicate by newspaper, radio, television, handbills, placards or other print, broadcast, telephone directory, or electronic medium.

KENTUCKY

Bottom Line: Advertising is Prohibited

Citation: Rev. Stat. § 199.590(1)

A person, corporation, or association shall not advertise in any manner that it will receive children for the purpose of adoption. A newspaper published, prepared, sold, or distributed in the Commonwealth of Kentucky shall not contain an advertisement that solicits children for adoption or solicits the custody of children.

LOUISIANA

Bottom Line: Advertising is Prohibited

Citation: Rev. Stat. § 46:1425(A)

It shall be unlawful for any person or organization other than a licensed child-placing agency or a Louisiana-based crisis pregnancy center to advertise through print or electronic media that it will adopt children or assist in the adoption of children.

MAINE

Bottom Line: Advertising is Prohibited

Citation: Rev. Stat. Tit. 18-A, § 9-313

A person may not:

- Advertise for the purpose of finding a child to adopt or to otherwise take into permanent physical custody.
- Advertise that the person will place a child for adoption or in any other permanent physical placement.
- Advertise for the purpose of finding a person to adopt or otherwise take into permanent custody a particular child.

This section does not prohibit:

- The Department of Health and Human Services or a child-placing agency from advertising in accordance with rules adopted by the department.
- An attorney licensed to practice in this State from advertising the attorney's availability to practice or provide services relating to the adoption of children.

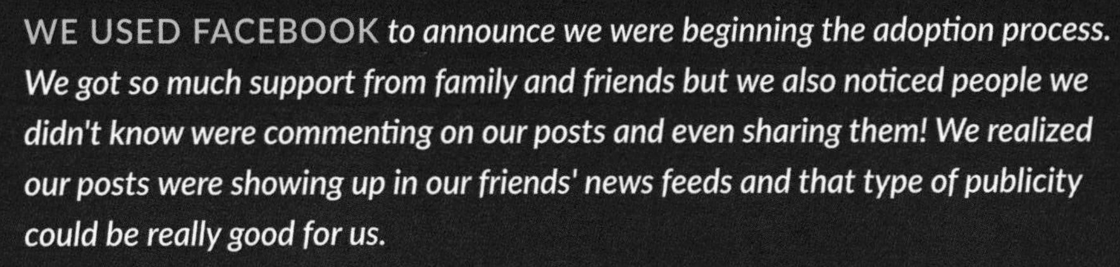

WE USED FACEBOOK *to announce we were beginning the adoption process. We got so much support from family and friends but we also noticed people we didn't know were commenting on our posts and even sharing them! We realized our posts were showing up in our friends' news feeds and that type of publicity could be really good for us.*

After a couple months we decided to step up our game and begin advertising on Facebook. At first we just did small things like boosting a post here or there, but at some point we got serious about it and started spending around $200 a month. It was crazy. Within a few months we had over 4,000 followers, and our boosted posts were reaching 1,500 people at a time.

After our third month of boosting posts we started getting contacts from expectant parents. Several were girls that just found out they were pregnant, and for those contacts we just had friendly conversations with them as their pregnancy progressed, but we didn't really think those would work out. We got close to an official "match" with someone but it fell apart. Out of nowhere one of the younger expectant moms reached out again, she was now 7 months along and sure of her plan. Our second son is due next month and we are thrilled!

LAWS BY STATE

Some guidelines on advertising in your state.

MARYLAND

Bottom Line: Advertising is Allowed

This issue is not addressed in the statutes reviewed.

MASSACHUSETTS

Bottom Line: Advertising is Prohibited

Citation: Ann. Laws Ch. 210, § 11A

It is unlawful for any person or entity other than a duly authorized agent or employee of the Department of Children and Families or a child care or child-placing agency licensed under the provisions of chapter 15D to cause to be published in the Commonwealth an advertisement or notice of children offered or wanted for adoption, or in any way offer to place, locate, or dispose of children offered or wanted for adoption, or hold himself or herself out in any way as being able to place, locate, or dispose of children for adoption.

MICHIGAN

Bottom Line: Advertising is Allowed

This issue is not addressed in the statutes reviewed.

MINNESOTA

Bottom Line: Advertising is Allowed

This issue is not addressed in the statutes reviewed.

MISSISSIPPI

Bottom Line: Advertising is Allowed

Citation: Ann. Code § 43-15-117

No child-placing agency shall advertise in the media markets in Mississippi seeking birth mothers or their children for adoption purposes unless the agency holds a valid and current license. Any child-placing agency, physician, or attorney who advertises for child-placing or adoption services in Mississippi shall be required by the division to show their principal office location on all media advertising for adoption services.

Nothing in this section precludes payment of reasonable medical, legal, or other lawful services fees, and for the legal proceedings related to lawful adoption proceedings; and no provision of this section abrogates the right of procedures for independent adoption as provided by law.

MISSOURI

Bottom Line: Advertising is Allowed

This issue is not addressed in the statutes reviewed.

MONTANA

Bottom Line: Advertising is Prohibited

Citation: Ann. Code § 42-7-105(1)(a)

No person, other than the Department of Public Health and Human Services or a licensed child-placing agency, may advertise in any public medium that the person knows of a child who is available for adoption, is willing to accept a child for adoption, or knows of prospective adoptive parents for a child.

NEBRASKA

Bottom Line: Advertising is Prohibited

Citation: Rev. Stat. § 43-701

Except as otherwise provided in the Nebraska Indian Child Welfare Act, no person other than a parent shall advertise a child for placement unless such person shall be duly licensed by the Department of Health and Human Services under such rules and regulations as the department shall prescribe.

NEVADA

Bottom Line: Advertising is Prohibited

Citation: Rev. Stat. § 127.283; 127.310(1)

No person or organization other than a licensed child-placing agency may advertise that he or she will place children for adoption or permanent free care; except, supply, provide, or obtain children for adoption or permanent free care; or cause any advertisement to be disseminated soliciting, requesting, or asking for any child or children for adoption or permanent free care.

NEW HAMPSHIRE

Bottom Line: Advertising is Allowed

Citation: Rev. Stat. § 170-E:39

A child-placing agency licensed or operating under a permit issued by the Department of Health and Human Services may publish advertisements of the services for which it is specifically licensed or issued a permit under this subdivision.

No person who is required to obtain a license or permit under this subdivision may advertise or cause to be published an advertisement soliciting or offering a child for placement unless the person has obtained the requisite license or permit.

NEW JERSEY

Bottom Line: Advertising is Allowed

This issue is not addressed in the statutes reviewed.

NEW MEXICO

Bottom Line: Advertising is Allowed

Citation: Ann. Stat. § 32A-5-42.2

This section does not apply to:

- The Children, Youth and Families Department or a person authorized to act on behalf of the department.
- An agency licensed by the department.
- An investigator or counselor.
- An attorney licensed in the State who advertises legal services relating to adoption.
- A prospective adoptive parent who is acting alone on the prospective adoptive parent's own behalf and who has a current, approved preplacement study as required by the department.

NEW YORK

Bottom Line: Advertising is Allowed

This issue is not addressed in the statutes reviewed.

NORTH CAROLINA

Bottom Line: Advertising is Allowed

Citation: Gen. Stat. § 48-10-101(b)-(b1)

No one other than a county department of social services, an adoption facilitator, or a licensed agency may advertise in any periodical or newspaper, or by radio, television, or other public medium, that any person or entity will place or accept a child for adoption.

This article shall not prohibit a person from advertising that the person desires to adopt. This section shall apply only to a person with a current completed preplacement assessment that finds the person suitable to be an adoptive parent.

The advertisement may be published only in a periodical or newspaper or on radio, television, cable television, or the Internet. The advertisement shall include a statement that:

- Indicates that the person has a completed preplacement assessment.
- Identifies the name of the agency that completed the preplacement assessment.
- Identifies the date the preplacement assessment was completed.
- States whether the person is willing to provide lawful expenses.

NORTH DAKOTA

Bottom Line: Advertising is Prohibited

Citation: Cent. Code § 23-16-08; 50-11-06; 50-19-11; 50-12-17

A person may not advertise, without a license to do so, in any public medium that the person knows of a child who is available for adoption or is willing to accept a child for adoption or that the person knows of prospective adoptive parents of a child.

LAWS BY STATE

Some guidelines on advertising in your state.

OHIO

Bottom Line: Advertising is Allowed

Citation: Rev. Code § 5103.17

The biological parent of a child may advertise the availability for placement of the parent's child for adoption to a qualified adoptive parent. A qualified adoptive parent may advertise that the qualified adoptive parent is available for placement of a child into the qualified adoptive parent's care for the purpose of adopting the child. A government entity may advertise about its role in the placement of children for adoption or any other information that would be relevant to qualified adoptive parents.

OKLAHOMA

Bottom Line: Advertising is Allowed

Citation: Ann. Stat. Tit. 21, § 866(A)(1)(g)-(h)

The crime of trafficking in children includes:

- Advertising of services for compensation to assist with the placement of a child for adoption by any person or organization, except by the department or a licensed child-placing agency.

- Advertisements for and solicitation of a woman who is pregnant to induce her to place her child upon birth for adoption, except by a licensed child-placing agency or an attorney.

Nothing in this section shall prohibit an attorney from the advertisement of legal services related to the adoption of children. Nothing in this section shall prohibit a person from advertising to solicit a pregnant woman to consider adoptive placement with the person or to locate a child for an adoptive placement into the person's own home, provided that such person has received a favorable preplacement home study recommendation in accordance with Â§ 7505-5.1 of Title 10, and that no money or other thing of value is offered as an inducement to the adoption.

OREGON

Bottom Line: Advertising is Allowed

Citation: Rev. Stat. § 109.311(4)

It is unlawful for any person to advertise a child offered or wanted for adoption or to advertise that the person is able to place, locate, dispose of, or receive a child for adoption. The provisions of this section do not apply to:

- The State Office for Services to Children and Families or a licensed Oregon adoption agency or an agent, employee, or person with whom the Office or adoption agency has a contract authorizing such actions.

- A person who has completed a home study and has received a favorable recommendation regarding the fitness of the person to be an adoptive parent or the person's attorney or uncompensated agent.

PENNSYLVANIA

Bottom Line: Advertising is Allowed

This issue is not addressed in the statutes reviewed.

RHODE ISLAND

Bottom Line: Advertising is Allowed

This issue is not addressed in the statutes reviewed.

PROFESSIONAL ADVICE FROM ADOPTHELP

THIS IS A STRESSFUL TIME, starting adoption outreach and waiting for a match. Please take care of YOU! Sleep late, plan vacations, take walks, indulge in a spa day–do whatever you can to pamper yourself. We want you to be mentally and emotionally ready when you receive the phone call that an expectant mother has selected you!

We also encourage our clients to reach out to support groups, spiritual or religious advisors, therapists, counselors or anyone else that can ease the wait time. You have been through quite the journey just to get started and you might need some help in finding your footing.

SOUTH CAROLINA

Bottom Line: Advertising is Allowed

Citation: Ann. Code. § 63-9-70

No person or entity other than the Department of Social Services, a child-placing agency licensed in this State, or an attorney licensed in this State may advertise that the person or entity will place or accept a child for adoption.

Notwithstanding the provisions above, a person is not prohibited from advertising that the person desires to adopt if the person has a current preplacement home investigation finding that the person is suitable to be an adoptive parent.

The term 'advertise' means to communicate by newspaper, radio, television, hand bills, placards or other print, broadcast, or electronic medium that originates within this State.

SOUTH DAKOTA

Bottom Line: Advertising is Allowed

This issue is not addressed in the statutes reviewed.

TENNESSEE

Bottom Line: Advertising is Allowed

Citation: Ann. Code. § 36-1-108(a)(2)

Only a licensed child-placing agency, a licensed clinical social worker, prospective adoptive parents, or a lawyer who is subject to the Tennessee supreme court rules regarding lawyer advertising may advertise for the placement of children for adoption in this State.

In order to advertise for the placement of children for adoption in Tennessee, out-of-State licensed child-placing agencies, licensed clinical social workers, or lawyers must:

- Be authorized to do business in this State under respective licensing laws.
- Maintain a physical office within this State or incur expenses involved in the transportation of a licensing consultant to the closest physical office of the agency, social worker, or lawyer.

Any advertisement in this State for the placement of children for adoption in another State by an agency or individual not licensed or authorized to do such business in this State shall clearly state that the agency or individual is not licensed or authorized to do such business in this State.

TEXAS

Bottom Line: Advertising is Prohibited

Citation: Penal Code § 25.09

A person commits an offense if the person advertises in the public media that the person will place a child for adoption or will provide or obtain a child for adoption. This section does not apply to a licensed child-placing agency that is identified in the advertisement as a licensed child-placing agency.

- It is legal to use outreach cards, networking letters, flyers in your personal outreach search.
- It is legal to have a blog, utilize social media, a website or YouTube.
- It is legal to use adoption parent profile websites.
- It is not legal to use traditional advertising media such as radio, billboards, television or Google Ads.

LAWS BY STATE

Some guidelines on advertising in your state.

UTAH

Bottom Line: Advertising is Prohibited

Citation: Ann. Code § 62A-4a-602(2)(b)

An attorney, physician, or other person may not:

- Issue, or cause to be issued, a card, sign, or device to any person indicating that he or she is available to provide child-placing assistance.
- Cause, permit, or allow any sign or marking on or in any building or structure indicating that he or she is available to provide child-placing assistance.
- Announce–or cause, permit, or allow an announcement–in any newspaper, magazine, directory, or on radio or television indicating that he or she is available to provide child-placing assistance.
- Advertise by any other means that he or she is available to provide child-placing assistance.

VERMONT

Bottom Line: Advertising is Allowed

This issue is not addressed in the statutes reviewed.

VIRGINIA

Bottom Line: Advertising is Allowed

Citation: Ann. Code § 63.2-1218; 63.2-1225

No person shall advertise or solicit to perform any activity prohibited by this section. Any person violating the provisions of this section shall be guilty of a felony.

A physician, attorney, or member of the clergy shall not charge any fee for recommending [a placement of a child for adoption] to a board or agency and shall not advertise that he or she is available to make such recommendations. An attorney may, however, charge for legal fees and services rendered in connection with the placement.

WASHINGTON

Bottom Line: Advertising is Allowed

Citation: Rev. Code § 26.33.400(1)-(2)

No person or entity shall cause to be published for circulation, or broadcast on a radio or television station, an advertisement of a child or children offered or wanted for adoption, or shall hold himself or herself out through such advertisement as having the ability to place, locate, dispose, or receive a child or children for adoption unless such person or entity is:

- A duly authorized agent, contractee, or employee of the department or a children's agency or institution, licensed by the department to care for and place children.
- A person who has a completed preplacement report with a favorable recommendation as to the fitness of the person to be an adoptive parent.

WEST VIRGINIA

Bottom Line: Advertising is Allowed

This issue is not addressed in the statutes reviewed.

WISCONSIN

Bottom Line: Advertising is Allowed

Citation: Ann. Stat. § 48.825

The term 'advertise' means to communicate by any public medium that originates within this State, including by newspaper, periodical, telephone book listing, outdoor advertising sign, radio, or television, or by any computerized communication system, including by electronic mail, Internet site, Internet account, or any similar medium of communication provided via the Internet.

The term 'Internet account' means an account created within a bounded system established by an Internet-based service that requires a user to input or store access information in an electronic device in order to view, create, use, or edit the users account information, profile, display, communications, or stored data.

No person may do any of the following:

- Advertise for the purpose of finding a child to adopt or to otherwise take into permanent physical custody.
- Advertise that the person will find an adoptive home or any other permanent physical placement for a child or arrange for or assist in the adoption, adoptive placement, or any other permanent physical placement of a child.
- Advertise that the person will place a child for adoption or in any other permanent physical placement.

This section does not apply to any of the following:

- The Department of Children and Families or a child welfare agency.
- An individual or agency providing adoption information.
- A foster care and adoption resource center.
- An individual who has received a favorable recommendation regarding his or her fitness to be an adoptive parent in this State.

No person may publish by a public medium an advertisement that violates this section. Nothing in this section prohibits an attorney licensed to practice in this State from advertising his or her availability to practice or provide services relating to the adoption of children.

WYOMING

Bottom Line: Advertising is Allowed

This issue is not addressed in the statutes reviewed.

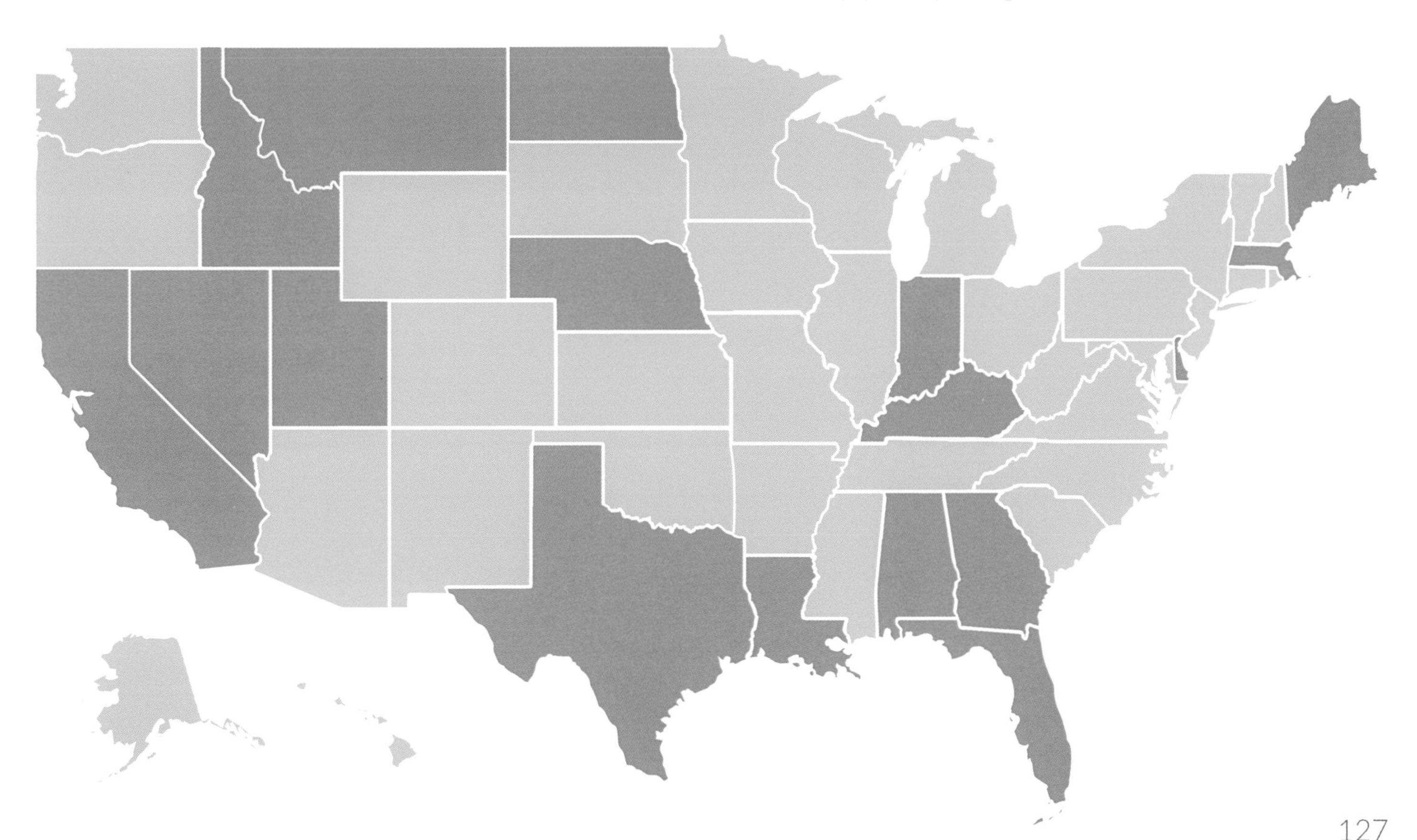

NOTES:

YOU'VE ADDED
TWO PIECES!

1 REVIEW YOUR STATE FOR AD LAWS 2 CONSULT ATTORNEY

THAT'S A WRAP!

TOPICS COVERED IN THIS SECTION:

- Thanks to Everyone Who Helped
- How to Get Even More Tips & Information for Free
- Our Completed Puzzle!

THANK YOU

We would like to thank the following people!

WE ARE SO GRATEFUL ***for all the families who were willing to share their stories and experience with us to help make this book a possibility. We would also like to thank all the social workers, agencies, attorneys and adoption professionals who looked over this book and contributed their knowledge and expertise to the project. And thanks to all the hard working team at Hopefully Parents that make this book a reality.***

TO OUR WONDERFUL CLIENTS

Thank you for sharing your stories, examples and your advice with others looking for help on their own adoption journey. There is nothing better than advice from someone who has already walked down this road:

- Shannon and Jonathan
- Chris and Troy
- John and Gidget
- John and Sarah
- Barry and Brittany
- Michael and Lisa
- Wes and Catherine
- Joel and Hillary
- Tim and Kelly
- Nik and Zach
- Laura and Kara
- Monte and Liz
- Mario and Clara
- Jason and Sharon
- Jason and James
- Andrew and Darci
- Ken and Lisa
- Jeff and Marjorie
- Seth and Stacey
- Elise and Angie

OTHER CONTRIBUTING AUTHORS

Thank you all for sharing your experience and advice with everyone reading this book. This is a more complete guide because of you!

- Hal Kaufman
- Tim Elder
- Amy Imber

INTERVIEWED FAMILIES

It takes extra time and effort to think through all of these questions and offer honest and thoughtful answers, so thank you! These interviews make the book a much richer reading experience.

- Brittany & Joe
- Heather & Brent
- Jessica & Josh
- Chris & Troy
- Hillary & Joel

BLUE DOG CREATIVE

Thank you to the amazing little family of Blue Dog Creative who strive to make each day beautiful. You guys are the best team anyone could hope for!

- Marcy Johnson
- Jennifer Morovic
- Evelyn Gruben
- Macey Nee
- Hailey Ayers
- Brad Klock
- Amanda Seed
- Kim Schaffer

BOOK EDITOR

John Crossman

NEED MORE INFO?

Additional resources, help and advice are available at our blog.

THE JOURNEY TO ADOPTION *can be a long and emotional road and, although it is always worth it in the end, sometimes we need help along the way. There are lots of resources available on the Hopefully Parents "Bright Ideas" blog. Be sure to check it out!*

BRIGHT IDEAS BLOG

Check out the Hopefully Parents "Bright Ideas" blog on our website for things like:

- Tip of the Week
- Additional Client Stories
- In-Depth Look at New Social Media Features
- Brainstorming 101 (New Ideas)
- **List of Additional Professional Resources**

HOPEFULLYPARENTS.COM/BRIGHTIDEAS

HOPEFULLYPARENTS.COM

WAY TO GO! ✓
YOU DID IT!

CONGRATULATIONS! YOU MADE IT TO THE END OF THE PUZZLE! APPLYING THE IDEAS FROM THIS BOOK INTO YOUR ADOPTION PLANS WILL HELP YOU COMPLETE YOUR OWN FAMILY PUZZLE. BEST OF LUCK ON YOUR JOURNEY!